Web-Based Learning:

A PRACTICAL GUIDE

Mary Ploski Seamon
and Eric J. Levitt

Linworth Publishing, Inc.
Worthington, Ohio

The authors would like to acknowledge Dr. Bernie Dodge, the original developer of the WebQuest concept. Details about Dr. Dodge's development of the concept can be found at <http://edweb.sdsu.edu/webquest/webquest.html>.

Cataloging-in-Publication Data

Seamon, Mary Ploski, 1943 –
    Web-based learning: a practical guide / Mary Ploski Seamon and Eric J. Levitt.
       p. cm.
    Includes bibliographical references and index.
    ISBN 1-58683-033-3 (perfectbound)
       1. Education—Computer network resources—Handbooks, manuals, etc. 2. Teaching—Computer network resources—Handbooks, manuals, etc. 3. Internet in Education—Handbooks, manuals, etc. I. Levitt, Eric J., 1970-II. Title.

LB1044.87 .S432001
371.33'4—dc21   2001029366

Published by Linworth Publishing, Inc.
480 East Wilson Bridge Road, Suite L
Worthington, Ohio 43085

ISBN 1-58683-033-3

5 4 3 2 1

Acknowledgments

Writing a book about changing instructional practices through technology training could not have been done without the continuing support, the perceptive comments, and the inspiring work of the teachers and administrators in Spartanburg (South Carolina) School District 3. The willingness of the teachers to experiment and to innovate in order to improve instruction continues to inspire us. We would like to give special thanks to the district superintendent, Dr. Jim Ray, who is a true visionary, and the Spartanburg School District 3 Board of Trustees, who wholeheartedly supported the commitment to implement a state-of-the-art technology program.

Without the love and support of our families, we would not have had the energy to complete this work. Our heartfelt gratitude goes to Eric's wife, Carmen, and Mary's son and daughter, Socrates and Trevor Seamon. We also would like to acknowledge the support and guidance of Mary's parents, Bill Ploski (deceased) and Mary Ploski, and Eric's parents, Arnold and Bonnie Levitt. We would like to extend a very sincere thank you to our editor, Judi Repman of Linworth Publishing, Inc., for her astute comments and encouragement.

About the Authors

Mary Ploski Seamon is a native of Connecticut and now resides in South Carolina. She is the mother of two children—Trevor of Los Angeles, California and Socrates of San Jose, California. Mary is a former English teacher, Assistant Principal, and Principal at D. W. Daniel High School in Clemson, South Carolina. She credits Dr. Jim Ray, Superintendent, Spartanburg School District 3, for creating the vision of technology integration.

Eric J. Levitt is a native of Long Island. Eric and his wife, Carmen, make their home in South Carolina. Eric taught high school Social Studies in Grapevine, Texas. For the past three years, he has been the Technology Trainer for Spartanburg School District 3 in South Carolina.

Contents

Contents *continued*

Contents *continued*

Contents *continued*

List of Figures

List of Figures continued

Introduction

If we don't change, we don't grow. If we don't grow, we aren't really living.

— Gail Sheehy

Everything is changing. It seems we don't have time to understand what we think is currently important before something else is important. Technology innovation takes place weekly—or maybe even daily and hourly. We know that slick wireless appliances will replace the computer. What then is the point of teaching students to use the computer? If you answered "no point," you are right. The computer is a means to an end. To worry that if we begin using computers in the classrooms new machines will replace them is foolhardy. Of course, they will—and new software will replace old software.

Change happens; it should not worry us. As educators, we understand that we are not teaching the technology itself or the software itself. We are teaching students to understand their world. Students must be actively engaged in their own learning. The best teachers are the ones who realize that their job is not putting in information—pouring knowledge into students' heads—but those teachers who understand that their job is helping students to use knowledge. By gathering the most relevant and current data available, students become information-literate. The importance of information literacy cannot be overstated. Information literacy is the fifth core subject.

Creating the Model

Three years ago, this book's co-author, Eric Levitt, and I met and began to plan computer training in a school district that had expanded technology rapidly. Eric, the newly hired technology trainer, came into my office with the standard books to teach Microsoft Outlook, the district e-mail program, and Microsoft Word.

"*I really want you to teach teachers to use the technology. You know, like WebQuests and other projects,*" I said, as I looked the manuals over with lukewarm approval.

Eric agreed readily—he was young and eager to please, after all.

I later learned that he went from my office and began checking out WebQuests. He didn't know what they were.

We were both naive. I mistakenly believed that in a 45-hour graduate course, teachers would be able to create a WebQuest easily; he thought I knew what I was talking about when I made the request.

But, in spite of it all, we bonded. Fortunately, I asked Eric to begin presenting with me at conferences. Presenting together forced us to make time in our busy schedules to begin talking—honestly—about how the training was going. About mid-year, we looked at the first of the teacher projects. Although they were interesting and useable, the projects were not WebQuests. Disappointed, we tried to pinpoint why the results we were getting were not what we had expected.

Eric shared that WebQuests intimidated teachers. When he showed the class Tom March's groundbreaking WebQuest, *Searching for China* **<http://www.kn.pacbell.com/wired/China/ChinaQuest.html>**, the class was dismayed—not excited. Just imagine that you have been sitting in an *introductory* computer course for about six weeks. Word processing and e-mail seemed doable, and Web pages were exciting, but a little bit out of reach. Then, like a clap of thunder, the instructor walks into the room and shows you the quintessential WebQuest and explains that creating one would be the next assignment. We looked at *Searching for China* again, this time through the eyes of someone who was new to computer use.

The bar was raised a little bit too high for them. We continued to talk. If we wanted teachers to succeed, which of course we did, then the bar would need to be adjusted. This decision did not mean that our expectations for what they could achieve was any lower, but simply that teachers needed immediate success in using technology in the classroom in order to continue to use technology. After all, who seeks out a new way to fail?

The Web-Based Learning Model was conceived. As with all conceptions, the idea grew slowly. Unhappy with the approach we were taking with the training, we knew there had to be a way to connect technology training to the higher-order thinking skills demanded by the accountability measures that have swept the country.

Did the model make sense to teachers? The teachers responded positively. We thought we had it. The birth was really the easy part. The next step was to raise the child. We worked over the next two years to raise the child correctly. We experimented; we changed; we became discouraged; we rejoiced.

While presenting at a conference last spring, we talked about the many failures that went into creating The Web-Based Learning Model. Eric laughed and pointed out that since he had fewer years of experience than I that he had fewer failures. We all laughed. But, he was correct. If we are risk takers—and most educators are—we can expect to add failures through the years. As successful educators, however, we had to take the failures and learn from them.

To be successful in integrating technology into classroom instruction, training for teachers must first focus on effective lesson plan design and teaching strategies. Without mastering these skills first, no amount of technical training, no matter how effective, will translate into valuable technology units.

Sequential Professional Development

If we want to make changes for students, we have to change the way we teach. The concept of changing instructional practices through technology training focuses on encouraging teachers to use technology to create an environment in which all students are challenged through a rigorous, rich classroom instructional program.

Group collaboration is a key component in using The Web-Based Learning Model successfully. Technology and curriculum standards are integrated into projects and simulations to allow students to apply their technology knowledge and skills within the context of the subject. Skills and strategies are taught in a meaningful context. Students interact and manipulate facts and concepts to transform their understanding. They become information-literate. Then, aware of the questionable nature of some Web sites, they have the ability to critically evaluate results. Teachers have guided students in knowing how to search.

We need to rethink our delivery of professional development and move away from the one-size-fits-all program. We must focus the staff development within the school so that we can build learning communities where teachers can support each other and ascertain that they are important, they are together, and they can tackle any problem. Ongoing assistance must be provided to get teachers through those first agonizing technology lessons where nothing seems to go right.

The chapters in this book are organized to allow the reader to see the entire process of technology integration. The emphasis is on the classroom teacher. It is practical. Classroom examples are contained throughout the book.

Chapters 4-6, 8 and 9 each feature a Technical Corner that gives a quick overview of the technical skills needed to develop or complete a Guided Tour, Scavenger Hunt, CyberInquiry, or WebQuest. The only skills that are presupposed are keyboarding and the ability to open a word processor or Internet browser. Readers who do not feel comfortable with their technical skills will appreciate the easy-to-use Appendix, which features a Technology Corner Matrix of Skills and more thoroughly discusses the technical skills mentioned in the text. Technical skills are organized by corresponding chapter to make the search easier. In addition, the Appendix provides an accompanying set of complete instructions on how to accomplish technical tasks, from copying and pasting to creating a Web page.

Chapters 4-9 each introduce one of the six process steps in The Web-Based Learning Model. The process steps are Guided Tour, Scavenger Hunt, Web Page, Internet Discovery, CyberInquiry, and WebQuest. Following the discussion of each process step, we provide sample lessons in the Exhibit Center. Several of the examples are threaded throughout the process steps to provide a common theme that demonstrates how the model builds from one step to another step.

The Exhibit Center offers examples that were designed and developed by teachers trained in The Web-Based Learning Model. Commentary sections after the exhibits discuss the strengths and weaknesses of each example and demonstrate that units evolve over time. As with all lesson planning, the units are revised and added to as more information becomes available, or as the teacher finds out what works and what doesn't work with students.

Notes to Trainers and Teachers

The Web-Based Learning Model is a sequential model that leads to a WebQuest. As we use the model for training, we have found that it is important to follow each process step. The reason is threefold. First, as the trainer works with the teacher or students through each process step, it establishes a common language. In some circles, for example, the term WebQuest has become so generic that it is used to mean any Web-based lesson plan. Second, since a Guided Tour is less complex than many of the later process steps, the teacher or student experiences immediate success. That success is important, particularly to teachers who are new users of technology. Third, the model builds in complexity. By following the model, the complexity of the WebQuest becomes attainable.

The guide is designed for technology trainers, media specialists and teachers to use in developing a training program for the integration of technology. It is designed so media specialists may use it independently or with teachers who would like to reinforce skills that they have learned in application classes. It may also be used by those brave souls who would prefer to strike out on their own; the examples and the commentaries may allow a highly motivated teacher or media specialist to use the book as a self-paced learning guide.

The model is teacher-tested. Teachers have said that it's like a road map, a way to get around. They also like the idea that they can begin using technology in the classroom immediately. The Web-Based Learning Model works much like a map for a novice traveler. It will provide direction. After we have traveled the route several times, the map won't be necessary. We will have found our way.

Rewards

In a sense, each time a group of teachers completes a Web-based project, there are feelings of accomplishment. Teachers who complete projects feel motivated that they can tackle the next project with greater confidence and skill. They also appreciate that these activities can be used in their classrooms immediately. At this point, the introduction of a more complex project becomes doable.

The students of these teachers see them in a different light. All of a sudden, students are working on material that challenges them in new and exciting ways. Their teacher doesn't seem as stuffy or uptight. Teachers who use technology instruction effectively are able to motivate their students to reach new levels of learning and understanding. Students recognize that they have something in common with their teachers—the ability and desire to use technology. This helps foster a sense of shared purpose in the learning process.

Through it all, we must be grateful to the teachers, the media specialists, and the technology coordinators—many of whom go unnoticed during the typical school year. They are the people who are working tirelessly in the trenches and who are laying the learning out for the 21st century. They are the true risk takers. They are our heroes.

— *Mary Ploski Seamon*
   Eric J. Levitt

Chapter 1

Computers Didn't Make It Easier

"Blessed are the flexible, for they shall not be bent out of shape."
— Anonymous

Education is going through a period of great change. And we all know that planned change is uncomfortable. Starting a new job, moving to a new house, even taking a vacation, while exciting and stimulating, all contain elements of doubt and anxiety. What if the job falls short of expectations, or the moving van arrives a day early (or delivers a day late), and what if the family trip turns out to be like Chevy Chase's *Family Vacation*? But we know that when we plan for change, we can find something good about it some of the time. After all, we made the *decision* to change. We have exercised some control.

The change imposed on us by technology has shaken us to our very core. Teachers are condemned for their lack of technical expertise. Those teachers, many of whom have long years of valued experience and have been considered proficient and able, are suddenly being asked to abandon (or so it seems) proven practices and to begin to experiment with computers.

The Big Lie

Could it be that we were misled, and we feel cheated? **Computers were supposed to make our lives easier.** Initially, technology promised to make us more productive and efficient. We could spend more time teaching our students. That wasn't true. We spent hours just learning to use the computer. But, we lost more than time. To add insult to injury, the tables turned, and our comfort zone shrank when we realized some students were much better at technology than we were. (Admit it; you have a student in mind right now.) He or she is the one who manipulates the keyboard and mouse in a fine ballet of speed, agility, and wild abandon. You shake your head in astonishment, wondering how they jump between Web sites, figure out every formatting feature in the word processor, and listen to music all within five minutes of sitting down in front of a computer.

"For goodness sakes…how am I going to figure out how to do that?" you think to yourself.

We can't help but worry as we embrace change. *Will we measure up to what is being expected of us? Can we prove to ourselves that we can make the adaptation and continue to be successful?* To move forward with technology change, we must provide teachers with the support and the caring necessary to assist them as they take the next step. We can't beat up the agents of change—the teachers—and expect them to embrace the technology without allowing time for new learning and personal support.

So, Right…Just Integrate!

With this dizzying image of students racing through the information superhighway and ignoring all of the red lights, you attend the first curriculum meeting of the year. Of course, the first item on the agenda requires you, the teacher, to integrate technology into your classroom. *GASP!*

Once oxygen is administered, and everyone has regained a little composure, the task looms large. There are more questions than answers.

"The district has invested big bucks. Get on board or else!"

In despair, we ask:

"How do you expect me to use computers in the classroom when I've got to teach all day?"

"Who is going to show ME how to use the computer?"

Questioning the value of technology, critics point to games and glitz as the real reason educators want to use computers. In many cases, computers become rather expensive paperweights sitting on classroom tables. In staff surveys, teachers indicate that they desperately want to be trained on how to use computers and technology for classroom instruction, but a combination of budget concerns, poor planning, and half-hearted implementation plans often neglect training as an imperative.

Feasibility

Targeted and continuous professional development must be implemented to provide teachers the support necessary to make the change. Since teachers have very few professional development days to devote to retraining, the training must take place "on the fly." Successful staff development models emphasize "just in time" professional development—providing training and support as it is needed by the teacher. We know that successful school reform comes from the classroom, not the central office. Therefore, the training must take place in the school setting with the equipment that the teacher will have available in the classroom. Further, the training must be directly related to what is taught in the classroom. Unless the teacher adopts the reform, classroom practices will not change. Before adoption takes place, there must be clear tasks and activities, accessible materials to use, and clear expectations of what is to come.

Changing the Way We Teach

What appears to be ignored in this great debate about technology is instructional practice. The computer provides a *means* to make the change—the computer itself is not the basis for the change. Effective computer use promotes *active learning*—that is, students collaborating, working together to solve different parts of the same problem, and producing a new way of looking at information. We will see teachers linking instruction and assessment, providing opportunities for students to develop portfolios, and providing opportunities for students to work on peer assessments. We will see media specialists helping teachers and students access informative Web sites that will add to the learning that is taking place in the classroom. Media centers continue to be the information hub.

Learning takes on depth, not breadth. We can expand the four walls of the classroom into the world. Changes in the learning environment, however, take time, support, and extended professional development.

Effective lesson design helps students explore ideas, acquire and synthesize information, and frame and solve problems. The creative problem solving, which depends upon context, interrelationships, and real-world activities, is available through Internet projects. If we examine state and local academic standards, we note that there is a reliance on the application of skills. Content knowledge must not be taught merely for the sake of learning facts but as a means to understand broader issues. Students must be able to research, analyze, and communicate information.

Make the Connection

The technology instruction must be directly related to what the teacher is teaching in the classroom. The professional development itself and how it is organized must make the connection between the classroom and the technology. In this age of high-stakes testing and academic standards, the training must be directly related to the standards-based curriculum that informs teaching in the content areas. We all agree that it is essential for teachers to expose students to higher standards, authentic learning experiences, multi-step processes, and creative, divergent thinking. The technology program must be designed to assist teachers in implementing the multi-step, creative, standards-based instruction by emphasizing the construction of interdisciplinary units that support the standards.

The technology training must be timely, relevant, and accessible to teachers. There must be a clearly delineated scope and sequence that scaffolds the adult learning from simple to more complex. If we ask that a teacher develop a WebQuest as an introductory technology training activity, we diminish the richness and complexity of the task.

Despite our natural tendency to resist unwanted change, we have managed over the past few years to devise strategies and methods that allow technology and good instructional practice to co-exist and to thrive. If we take the time to examine real-world experiences, we can paint a clearer picture of how technology can become a welcome visitor rather than an unwanted freeloader.

Challenges

The challenges we face in K-12 education are enormous. Many states have adopted new academic standards that are connected to accountability and high-stakes testing. As the national move to raise standards and expectations for students accelerates, educators are forced to question what we believe about students and learning. We are all very quick to state that we believe that all students can learn. Our view of the potential of students, however, is constrained by the very structure of schools. Resources are limited. Furthermore, faced with conservative budget increases, media centers are limited in the materials that can be purchased by the soaring prices of print media. Although most educators believe that students have diverse learning styles, very little can be done to accommodate these differences in the traditional classroom or with the current resources.

This is not new stuff. As early as 1916, John Dewey contended that we learn by doing. Since then, we have been struggling with how to accomplish that in the core curriculum.

Motivation and Praise

In order to successfully change instruction through technology training, certain factors need to be present. As in any educational environment, the learners need to have motivation. How does one motivate adult learners who are reticent about stepping into the technology arena? Praise and patience go a long way in getting people to wade into unfamiliar and intimidating waters. All too often, we hear tales from teachers about computer courses that they have taken. Their stories are strikingly similar and sound something like this:

"I took a word processing class one time, but the instructor made everyone feel about two inches tall."

Learning to use technology to transform teaching practices takes time. With a computer-phobic teacher, a typical three-hour graduate credit course will not change instructional practices. The teacher may begin using the computer for productivity but may not have mastered the skills necessary to use it with students.

Best Practices

The traditional model of teaching places the teacher at the front and center of the classroom with all desks facing in one direction. The teacher lectures, wisdom and knowledge get picked up by the students, and "poof," learning occurs. But what happens when we ask the teacher to drastically alter this method of teaching and to become a facilitator rather than the "sage on the stage"?

The idea of "teacher as facilitator or guide" is not new. Knowing more about attention spans and learning styles, teachers who incorporate best practices routinely remove themselves from the spotlight and allow students to create and construct their own learning. Why then, has the teacher as facilitator model met with such resistance when it comes to integrating technology into the curriculum?

Through integration of technology, we have the opportunity to develop a framework of information that provides the stepping stones necessary for all students to develop the requisite skills and critical thinking necessary for them to be successful. It has been well documented through brain research that learners get greater understanding from learning if they are allowed to freely interact with and transform the learning to new practices and new ways of thinking. Also, we understand that learning moves from working memory to long-term memory when sense and meaning are connected to the learning. In other words, if we can accept the learning as important, then we will retain it. Or, if we can make sense of that learning, we will retain it. Learning occurs most powerfully when we can understand something and then use it. If we understand where it fits in the real world, we will remember it more easily. The problem solving available through Web-based applications—through real world simulations—is a fertile ground for this to occur.

In order to accomplish this, the structure of the classroom must change. We need to view the computer in the classroom as a group-work center, a place in which the students work in teams, reinforcing the skills and competencies necessary to complete a task or a simulation. Instead of one teacher and 25 students, we transform the classroom into an environment that supports and encourages the students to be teachers and the teachers to be learners. Teachers who are fortunate to have a cluster of computers in the classroom can make the classrooms learner-centered.

When we talk about changing the classroom, the reason for the change becomes obvious. Students learn best when given information in multiple formats. Although a lecture is excellent for presenting information quickly, it is only 10 percent successful in helping a student retain information after 24 hours. If they see and hear it, students are 20 percent more likely to retain the information. Not surprisingly, a student retains 80 percent of the information if allowed to practice by doing. The actual teaching of a concept helps the student to retain 90 percent of what is learned. Consider the implications. If we place students in heterogeneous groups, working on a problem, after we have presented the basic facts that they need to interact with the material, they are very likely to retain the new information. Collaboration and teamwork foster the highest levels of retention.

The Bottom Line

The bottom line is that we all need to take some risks, endure some failures, and feel uncomfortable for a while in order to successfully change instruction.

Our world values flexibility, innovations, self-direction, and collaborative problem solving. Harold Wenglinsky, Educational Testing Service, in *Does It Compute? The Relationship Between Educational Technology and Student Achievement in Mathematics* observes that "eighth graders whose teachers used computers mostly for simulations and applications—generally associated with higher-order thinking—performed better on NAEP [National Assessment of Educational Progress] tests than students whose teachers did not. In both fourth and eighth grades, students whose teachers had professional development with computers outperformed students whose teachers didn't." (Wenglinsky, available online: **<http://www.ets.org/textonly/aboutets/news/00101301.html>**). Wenglinsky, in fact, says he was struck by the fact that any amount of professional development translated into student achievement gains.

The Model

It's time to forge forward. In the next chapter we will introduce a model for professional development that prepares a teacher to use Web-based learning to change instructional design. Chapter 3 will focus on the development of the essential question, a core element in the development of the lessons that follow.

This book offers a straightforward framework for integrating technology into classroom instruction. After three years of feedback, modifications, and constant self-analysis, we believe that any school or district that has not yet implemented a technology training plan, or that intends to re-evaluate its current plan, will find this book both useful and enjoyable. The Web-Based Learning Model provides a sequential model for professional development.

Chapter 2

The Framework for Change

"I'm not young enough to know everything."
— *J. M. Barrie*

What are the persistent challenges we face as we try to integrate technology into the classroom? One of the most persistent challenges is the time and energy we spend learning how to use technology effectively with students. Experienced teachers who lack the technical savvy of their students can change their instructional practice. Sometimes, though, when we introduce something new, we have to give something up.

If we use computer instruction to enrich classroom practices, we must reintegrate what we teach to make room in our curriculum for active student involvement with a curriculum of depth, not breadth. Teachers need to use technology within the content in which they are most comfortable. As a teacher expands his or her comfort zone, training should spiral upward to deeper content and higher sophistication. Teachers need to master the integration in a way that works for them individually. Whether the initial forays involve downloading multimedia projects created by other teachers or adding a technology element into a "regular" classroom lesson, a teacher's use of technology should be encouraged.

If At First You Don't Succeed

Unfortunately, the axiom "If at first you don't succeed, try and try again" is not widely accepted when it comes to professional development for teachers. School districts pay big money for instructors to model relevant and proven techniques for their teachers. As educators we know that learning occurs over time—and occurs best when we are given an opportunity to practice—but the focus of professional development seems to be on what can be learned (or taught) in a six-hour format. There usually is not a great deal of patience or tolerance for a program that may take several years to become truly useful and practical. As fast as change happens, who can expect the staff developer or the principal to be around that long?

Nevertheless, professional development must be thought of as a process—not an event. As with any process, an introduction is necessary. "Guest" speakers have a place in this process but cannot be viewed as the whole show. After the initial presentation, professional development must continue. Teachers must have an opportunity to experiment with technology in a non-threatening environment. The initial first steps must be encouraged. Support, through ongoing professional development, must be available to the teacher in the classroom. Through effective professional development and teacher commitment to incorporating the best teaching practices in all modes of classroom instruction, technology integration can be an effective new method of instruction.

Improved Instruction

In order to accomplish the goal of improved instruction, technology training must focus on two primary areas of emphasis:
1. Giving teachers the technical skills necessary to interact with knowledge and construct the information.
2. Providing teachers with the expertise to develop simulations and activities that engage students.

In order to provide an effective model for professional development, we have incorporated core knowledge requirements into a six-step process called **The Web-Based Learning Model**. The model takes a teacher through a sequential program that involves creating classroom applications of increasing difficulty. The six process steps build on each other and demonstrate how to use the World Wide Web as an information source to extend student learning.

The Six Process Steps

The basis of the model is that computer skills can be learned best when the teacher sees the classroom application and the benefit to students. Consequently, the instruction evolves through classroom applications that build upon one another in **six process steps: Guided Tour, Scavenger Hunt,**

Web Page, **Internet Discovery**, **CyberInquiry**, and **WebQuest**. The amount of material and knowledge increases from one process step to another. Teachers (and students) also need higher technical skills as they move from one process step to the next. The advantage of progressing through each process step is that the teacher can immediately begin using technology in the classroom. A Guided Tour, for example, can be constructed overnight and used the next day in class.

In the beginning stage, the teacher works through each step, building the technical skills needed. In the advanced stage, the teacher is comfortable with the concept and can work back and forth among the process steps, much as we do with all things. Figure 2.1 presents the Web-based learning framework.

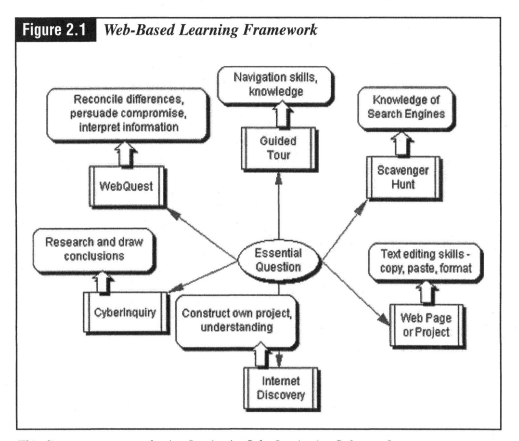

Figure 2.1 *Web-Based Learning Framework*

This diagram was created using Inspiration® by Inspiration Software, Inc.

During training, before we begin concentrating on the process steps, we ascertain the level of understanding that the teachers have about organizing instruction around an **essential question**. An essential question requires students to evaluate. Often referred to as the "big" questions, they force students to think at the highest levels of Bloom's Taxonomy, prodding students to construct their own meaning.

Process Step 1 is the Guided Tour. A Guided Tour is a teacher-developed or student-developed activity related to an instructional unit. The teacher identifies an introductory concept or a summary of facts for students to use individually or in groups and researches Web links that relate to the topic. The teacher asks questions that the students respond to by exploring the designated site(s). A teacher new to the Web may depend on **hotlists** (collections of links to Web sites) like the kind available at wonderful sites such as Blue Web'n **<http://pomo.kn.pacbell.com/wired/blueWebn/>** and Web **and Flow <http://www.Web-and-flow.com/>**. A Guided Tour is excellent for beginning technology users since it requires basic skills for the creator (e.g., copy and paste) and only navigation skills for the student user. Frequently, Guided Tours are used for introductory units and concepts or for review of learning.

Process Step 2 is the Scavenger Hunt. A Scavenger Hunt focuses on a particular theme or concept that the teacher is introducing or reviewing. To design a Scavenger Hunt, a teacher constructs questions that relate to a topic being studied. To participate in a Scavenger Hunt, a student needs to be able to effectively search the Web for information. After being taught to use a search engine and to identify key words to use in a search, a student can begin searching for sites on the Web to use in the collection of information.

Process Step 3 is the Web Page. At the introductory level, the Web Page or Web Project is a place to post student work or projects. In its simplest form, it summarizes a topic that a class has studied. Web Pages or Web Projects require basic word processing skills, including the ability to create tables. Using Microsoft Word, Netscape Composer or Gold (free for educators), or a program such as MS FrontPage (FrontPage Express is free), a student may create a Web Page or Project without any knowledge of HTML (Hypertext Markup Language, which the computer code used for creating Web pages).

Process Step 4 is the Internet Discovery. An Internet Discovery is student-originated research that is teacher-directed. The discovery itself is not the product; rather, it is the beginning step of a student-originated research paper, PowerPoint Show, Guided Tour, Web Page, CyberInquiry, or WebQuest.

Before a student is given the freedom for this activity, the teacher should feel confident that the individual is able to navigate, search, word process, evaluate information accurately, create Web pages, and use time wisely in the quest for information. Obviously, these are skills that any reflective student would need to have for effective research.

Process Step 5 is the CyberInquiry. The CyberInquiry is shaped in a similar fashion to a WebQuest *(see Process Step 6)*; however, a CyberInquiry project is more linear. It involves an introduction, investigation, gathering and sorting, portfolio, sharing, and evaluation. The teacher provides background material for the investigation, and the student generates additional research on the topic on the Internet. Because a CyberInquiry tends to be more linear than a WebQuest, it is simpler for a teacher to create.

A CyberInquiry requires the teacher to have more advanced technical skills than the previous projects because the development of the CyberInquiry requires a teacher to use all of the technical skills achieved up to this point.

Process Step 6 is the WebQuest. A WebQuest challenges students to explore the Web. Developed in 1995 by Bernie Dodge of San Diego State University (For more information, see **<http://edweb.sdsu.edu/EdWeb_ Folder/courses/EDTEC596/About_WebQuests.html>**), WebQuests generally encourage students to explore a topic in great depth. Most WebQuests include the links that are appropriate for students to research as well as provide suggestions for further research. WebQuests are generally constructed around a scenario of interest to students. Traditionally, WebQuests have an introduction, a process, a task, a list of resources, a conclusion, and an evaluation. The technical skills required to create a WebQuest are very similar to those required for a CyberInquiry.

Training and the Model

We have discovered that the model will work in any well-developed professional development program. Teachers prefer different formats for professional development, just as students prefer multiple formats when they are learning new information. The model has provided us with the basis for a three-credit-hour graduate course structured around the traditional 45 hours. We have structured individual parts of the model into one-graduate-hour courses. Often, we have presented the Web page design module in after-school workshops so faculty members can create their own Web pages in a supportive learning community. We have brought in guest experts to reinforce the learning and frequently have asked teachers and media specialists how they wanted the model to be delivered.

The most important—and the most intensive—part of the training has been the one-on-one training provided to the teachers. Teachers, even those who are most skittish about technology, are more willing to take a risk if someone is available to assist them in the very first lesson. A technology lead teacher, a media specialist, a technology trainer, or the next-door-neighbor teacher (if he or she is computer-literate) can provide this one-on-one training. The one-on-one approach depends more on support and caring rather than on sophisticated technical skills. We need to be nurtured as we learn new ideas.

As we provide the training (in whatever format is selected), we model the behavior we expect the teacher to exhibit while working with students when facilitating the student creation of a Guided Tour, a Scavenger Hunt, and ultimately a WebQuest. Teachers work in groups, sharing with one another. The framework builds so the material used to create the lower level models—Guided Tour or Scavenger Hunt—will lead to a WebQuest. By working in groups, the teachers also focus on developmentally appropriate lessons. An early childhood teacher, for example, would not aspire to the levels of abstract thought a CyberInquiry or a WebQuest requires of students. Instead, a group of early childhood teachers might incorporate visual clues and sequential patterns into a Guided Tour.

With each process step, there is a slight difference. The difference between a Scavenger Hunt and a Guided Tour is simple but critical. In a Guided Tour, the links are provided; in a Scavenger Hunt, the student searches for the links, usually in response to a question that a teacher may pose. The Internet Discovery is also a search for information. In the Discovery, the student knows enough information about the subject that he or she is able to frame a question and research additional information that answers the question. Likewise, the main difference between a CyberInquiry and a WebQuest is that the CyberInquiry does not depend upon roles that students enact. Rather, there is one task that must be completed. The chief characteristic of a WebQuest is that it generally incorporates several roles that may be in conflict in solving the problem.

The overall differences among the process steps are more complex than the functional differences just described. Each task requires a greater commitment to the role of "teacher as facilitator." With the Guided Tour, a teacher is able to tightly control the extent to which a student interacts with the information presented. By preselecting and prescreening Web sites that students will visit, the teacher determines what information students need. Through a series of questions—generally specific to the site—the teacher guides the students. The Scavenger Hunt, on the other hand, provides students with a basic question on a subject and asks that the student find information through a Web search. In order to be successful, the student must have a basic knowledge of the subject and the ability to use a search engine. Most important, the student must be able to critically assess the information at the Web site.

As teachers move through the six-step process, they must be comfortable scaffolding assignments. As students work in heterogeneous groups, the tasks that they are completing must allow for differences in computer ability, learning styles, multiple intelligences, motivation, and dedication.

The Web-Based Learning Model evolves through each process step; a teacher learns the technology skills necessary to develop a project, activity, or simulation to use in the classroom. Eventually, the teacher becomes comfortable moving back and forth among the process steps. However, until the teacher's comfort zone expands, the model should be followed closely.

The Training Framework

The Web-Based Learning Model works when the necessary professional development component is established. The most obvious way to acquire new skills is to provide the training necessary for the skills to be practiced. The model is a logical sequence of training content that is framed in the same way that we wish classroom instruction to take place. Working in interdisciplinary or grade-level teams, teachers create projects that they can use in their classrooms. As they work in the groups, they are modeling the behavior that they will use in their own classrooms, moving from whole-class to individual or group instruction. Each project requires that a teacher identify the curriculum or academic standards that are being taught through the project and create a rubric to assess that knowledge.

The Jigsaw

The Web-Based Learning Model lends itself well to a very active and effective learning model—the Jigsaw. Many teachers use Jigsaws with students in order to encourage independent learning as well as to narrow the topic that is covered into a more easily accomplished task. In a Jigsaw, a general topic is divided into smaller pieces. Each student or group of students selects one area in which they will become the experts. Each student researches and analyzes the information on that specific topic and returns to the smaller group. Each student, in turn, teaches the other students the part of the information that he or she has become expert in during the research phase.

Organization of Jigsaw learning is easy. The teacher takes the essential question and separates it into four smaller slices of information or concepts. The teacher then divides the class into four groups in which students research their information using articles, the Internet, and other related materials. Each student or group of students will later return to the original group as the "expert" on that aspect. This occurs after they have fully discussed the information among themselves and fully understand it. The teacher facilitates the exchanges by listening to the various groups and making suggestions for further research when necessary.

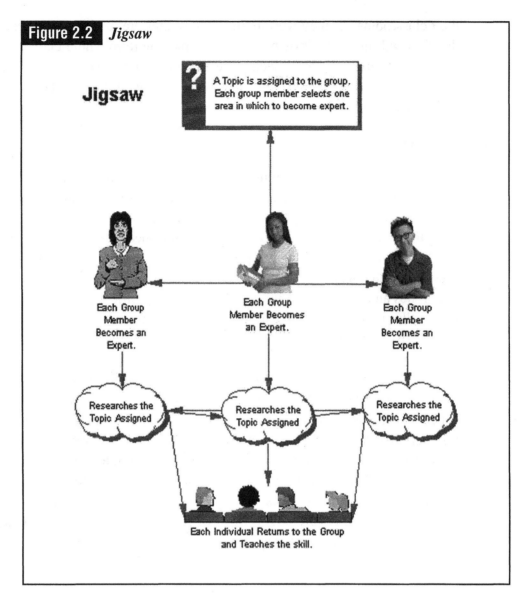

Figure 2.2 *Jigsaw*

This diagram was created using Inspiration® by Inspiration Software, Inc.

The entire concept of the Jigsaw fits in well with the belief that as teachers (and as learners) we need to organize information if we hope to remember it and, thus, use it. In using a Jigsaw with teachers, we may break down the particular skills needed for a project into smaller pieces. For example, a Guided Tour can be divided into essential question, hotlists, questions, and extended activities.

During training, we divide teachers into learning teams and then ask that each teacher become an expert in a particular part of the puzzle (activity). The learning teams may be formed by grade level, subject area, or technical expertise. The teacher who is most familiar with search engines may conduct the search for information; this person often is the media specialist. The media specialist would then teach the group how that skill is accomplished most effectively.

The Mentor

The training must provide multiple opportunities for teachers to be supported by a mentor or a trainer in the classroom as they begin the new instruction. Teachers should invite mentors in when they are feeling competent—as well as when they need the personal support. How do we find these mentors? In many cases, they are in the schools. Media specialists can provide the mentoring if they are given the time and the training. In other cases, additional staff will need to be added. Curriculum coordinators should be retrained to include technology implementation skills if they currently do not have those skills. We need to get past the idea that technology is an add-on or a peripheral part of "good" teaching.

If we do not provide these follow-up opportunities, the technical skill that the teacher has developed in training will not make a lasting difference in the classroom practice. The Web-Based Learning Model requires that the teachers begin skill development, practice in the classroom, return for additional skill development, and eventually become a skilled practitioner. If we are to visualize the professional development component of how training is organized, we see that to become a confident practitioner, a teacher must move from skill development to the classroom adaptation of the skill. What good is it to learn to navigate on the Web if a teacher never intends to use the skill again?

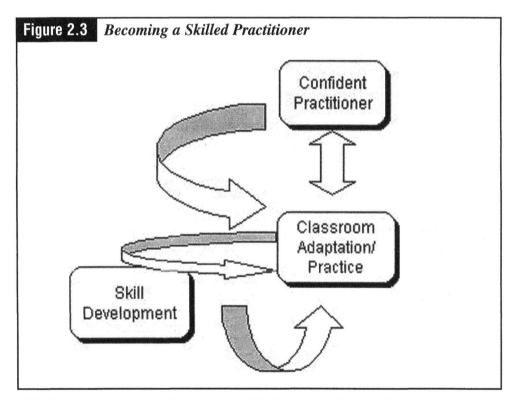

Figure 2.3 *Becoming a Skilled Practitioner*

This diagram was created using Inspiration® by Inspiration Software, Inc.

The professional development component requires that as the teacher learns the technology skills, opportunities are provided to successfully implement technology integration in the classroom. In this digital age, we are all accustomed to things happening quickly. Fast-paced and energetic, our students sweep past us in a blur. If we allow this to become a detractor in what we know is good instructional practice and design, we will have succumbed.

Chapter 3

The Essential Question

"Good teaching is more a giving of right questions than a giving of right answers."
— *Josef Albers*

Before we start to ask questions, we have to determine the key concepts—that is, the essence—of a lesson. Some days it is just easier to plow ahead and not worry about key concepts. How can we find the time to stop and ask what it is that we want students to learn? We are comfortable in our role as questioner. In other words, since teachers are good answerers, we assume we are good questioners.

And we are. We can fire staccato bursts of questions in rapid-fire sequence. But do those questions force us to think, to examine, to wonder, and to explore? Or do they ask us to remember? **Essential questions** require reflection by the student to answer, and they require reflection by the teacher to create. The time that a teacher takes to write a question that spirals the learning is time saved from more tedious review. A question that spirals learning builds from the student's previous learning and connects to an application of that learning.

In teaching a unit related to the Holocaust, a teacher might ask, *"Who wrote Anne Frank?"* to check for factual recall. Or the teacher may ask students to describe the room in which the Franks hid. But to extend the check for understanding to include perspective about the Holocaust, the teacher may try to capture the student's imagination, forcing the student to confront these very poignant questions: *"What did the Holocaust mean to the world?"* *"Were the victims of the Holocaust heroes?"*

The compelling part of any essential question is that it can be answered only if we apply our knowledge—a knowledge melded from many sources and subject areas. Essential questions thrive in an environment of simulations. What does the essential question do, and why is it so important to lesson planning? The essential question shapes our response to information. Essential questions prod teachers and students to evaluate, establishing a context for the content. Major issues, problems, concerns, interests, or themes are fertile content for essential questions. Questioning causes us to identify the problem that needs solving. Furthermore, essential questions serve as guideposts for what is taught and how it is assessed.

What is very important to teachers and to students is that the more complex the response demanded by a question, the more likely we are to see an increase in student achievement. After all, a question that scaffolds learning requires that a student be able to understand the information, to interpret the information, to apply the information, and then to transform the information by using it in a new way. The essential question must be *identified* before a student can do any of those things. Through the essential question, the student moves from collecting facts to shaping the information. An essential question compels a student to ponder the real life application of material and to move from content to context.

Essential questions have no correct answers; they are not black-and-white. Rather, an essential question moves a student to ponder the real life application of material and transform it by reacting to it, changing it, and reinventing it—content to context. The teacher, on the other hand, moves from concept and topic to the essential question. After those ideas are framed, the teacher defines the specific connections to the curriculum standards.

Often, using a graphic organizer program encourages teachers to freely brainstorm ideas on a topic. The free association helps teachers define essential questions. The diagram shown in Fig. 3.1 was created as teachers worked to define an essential question to use in a middle school interdisciplinary project. The teachers very quickly determined that the interdisciplinary unit they wanted to focus on was Earthquakes. But how to connect the social studies standards, English standards, and math standards was not clear to the teachers in the beginning. Consequently, they brainstormed.

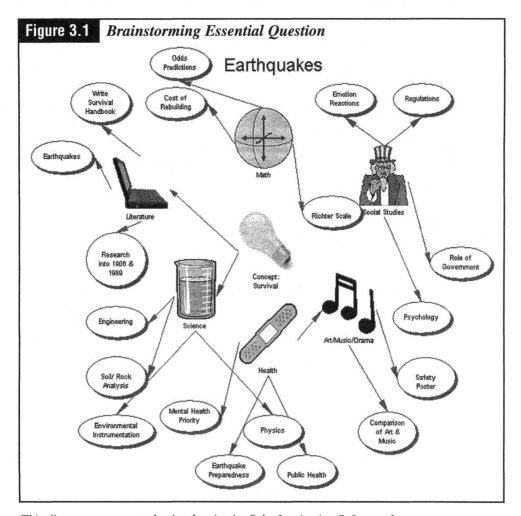

This diagram was created using Inspiration® by Inspiration Software, Inc.

If You Don't Say What You Mean...

We need to be clear when asking questions. If you don't say what you mean, you'll never mean what you say. The same holds true when we are defining essential questions. If the question is ambiguous and ill-defined, how will the students respond? Why is defining the essential question so difficult? For starters, it forces the instructor to define the learning goal very early in the process. The essential question reverberates through all of the activities and sets the tone for the learning that should take place.

Working with a team of middle school teachers who were developing an interdisciplinary unit using technology proved to be an eye-opener. During the summer, we met with one of the teachers to begin discussing ideas for a unit that would culminate in a WebQuest. One of the first mistakes we made was trying to "come up" with topics that were controversial. In the beginning, we did not allow the curriculum to naturally influence the topic and essential question for the unit. Instead, we looked at WebQuests on the Internet and tried in vain to generate a "hot topic" that was debatable and relevant.

At the next meeting with the team, we unveiled our ideas for a topic. The topics were broad: welfare reform, social security, genetic engineering, cloning, utopia, women in professional sports, athletes as role models, and salaries paid to professional athletes. The topics were also scattered and lacked focus. Being good teachers, however, they realized that they needed to bring the lesson back to standards, and they began to review the subject area academic standards. After a rather lengthy discussion, one of the topics began to take shape into something that could be taught by all three of the teachers in an interdisciplinary unit. *(See Figure 3.2.)*

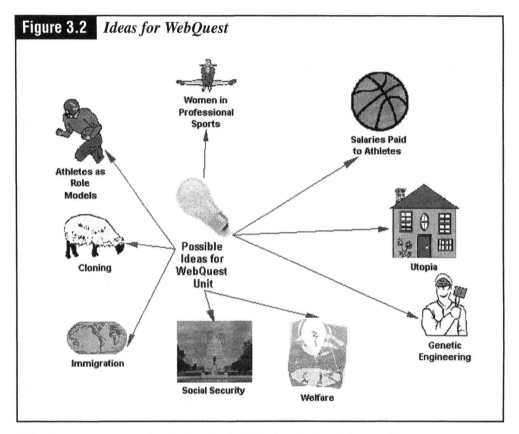

| Figure 3.2 | *Ideas for WebQuest* |

This diagram was created using Inspiration® by Inspiration Software, Inc.

Defining the Essential Question

The topic dealing with salaries paid to professional athletes began to take hold as the frontrunner for this unit. On the surface, it appealed to the teachers because the topic was timely, their students were interested in sports, and there was a good likelihood that Internet resources would be plentiful. More important, each teacher saw different strands and objectives that would be addressed by teaching this unit.

The essential question, however, remained undefined. After a few more rejections, the following question emerged: *"How should the salary of a professional athlete be structured?"* This question seemed so simple, but it was woven with just the right amount of complexity. There were no "yes" or "no" answers to this question. Students would somehow be required to develop a plan or proposal to determine how an athlete's salary should be structured.

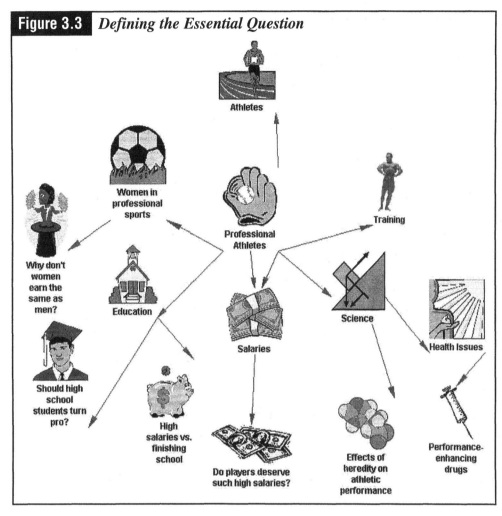

Figure 3.3 *Defining the Essential Question*

Athletes

Women in professional sports

Why don't women earn the same as men?

Education

Professional Athletes

Training

Science

Health Issues

Salaries

Should high school students turn pro?

High salaries vs. finishing school

Do players deserve such high salaries?

Effects of heredity on athletic performance

Performance-enhancing drugs

This diagram was created using Inspiration® by Inspiration Software, Inc.

After much trial and error, we decided that teachers needed a game plan to keep them focused as they crafted an essential question for the first time. Over time, we developed graphing examples that we used to demonstrate to teachers the brainstorming necessary to get to essential questions. Teachers worked in interdisciplinary teams (or occasionally they worked in grade-level or subject-area teams) and generated ideas about unit topics that could be used across interdisciplinary lines. Again, this is an area in which media specialists excel. Having a media specialist facilitate the group work is a tremendous benefit.

To structure the experience for teachers, we began to use an Essential Question Template that focused the teachers on the unit and topic they were teaching. Furthermore, we provided them with a framework to generate ideas related to the topic. As shown in Figure 3.4, the groups were encouraged to come up with a topic/unit that they wished to teach and to brainstorm related concepts.

Figure 3.4 *Essential Question Template*

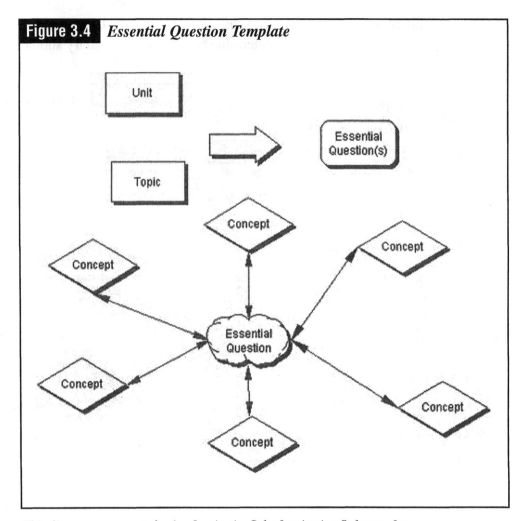

This diagram was created using Inspiration® by Inspiration Software, Inc.

Using the framework, we provided teachers with an example so they would be able to visualize how to work through the brainstorming session. In order to structure this experience for teachers, we generally followed a pattern. During the class introduction, we discussed essential questions. Some teachers had become very accustomed to planning their lessons around essential questions, and we encouraged them to discuss the techniques they had used in framing questions. We then structured the class so teachers would generate an essential question to be used throughout the course to develop the Web projects—from Guided Tours to WebQuests.

As teachers brainstormed ideas, they filled in the template. Although they would eventually plan what information was needed to develop the topic and discuss where to get the information and the resources to use, we emphasized that the essential question must come first. Brainstorming on several different ideas, teachers developed ideas for essential questions. Figures 3.5 through 3.7 emphasize a recycling waste unit, a unit on the Vietnam War, and one on music composition.

As you look at each example, notice that the essential question provides an umbrella under which a teacher would explore various other topics. In working with the idea of recycling waste, the essential question is *"Why don't people place a higher premium on conserving natural resources?"* The brainstorming leads into many areas—hazardous waste, health, and business opportunities.

Figure 3.5 *Recycling Waste by Doug Purinton, Broome High School*

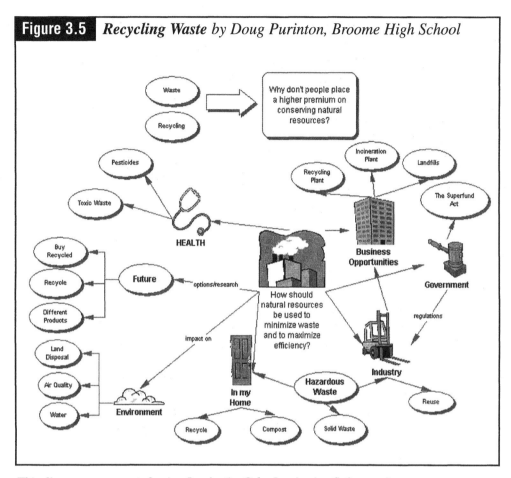

This diagram was created using Inspiration® by Inspiration Software, Inc.

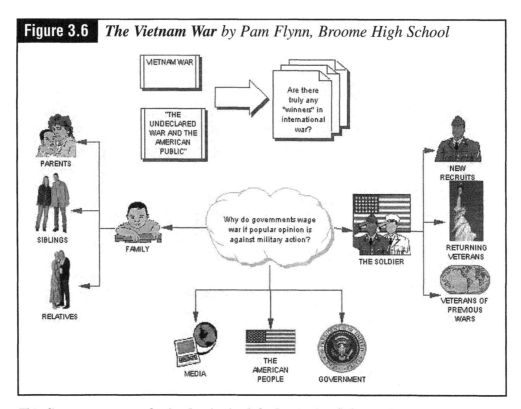

Figure 3.6 *The Vietnam War by Pam Flynn, Broome High School*

This diagram was created using Inspiration® by Inspiration Software, Inc.

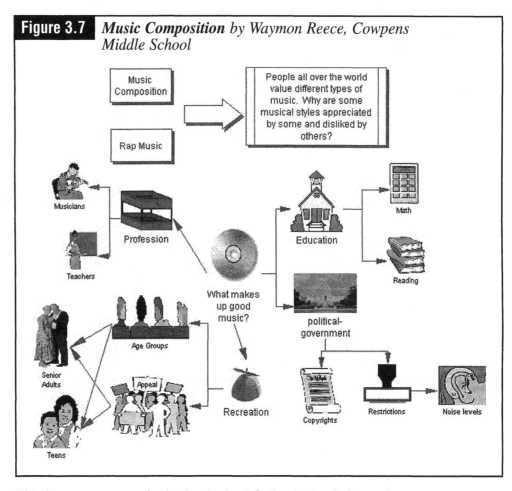

Figure 3.7 *Music Composition by Waymon Reece, Cowpens Middle School*

This diagram was created using Inspiration® by Inspiration Software, Inc.

The essential question must focus on a topic that is broad enough to offer several options for completing the work. In the sample math lesson shown in Figure 3.8, we emphasized that the completed lesson was only one variation of the essential question.

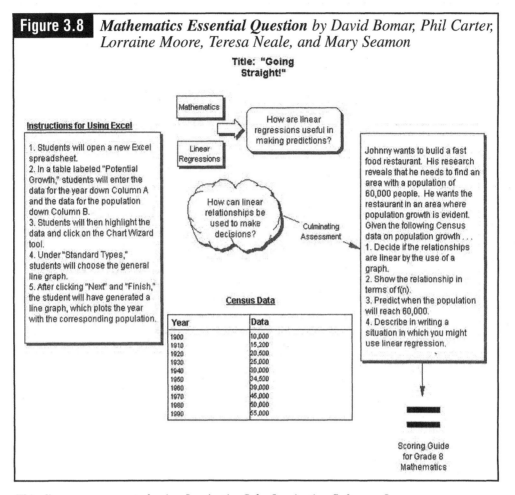

Figure 3.8 *Mathematics Essential Question by David Bomar, Phil Carter, Lorraine Moore, Teresa Neale, and Mary Seamon*

This diagram was created using Inspiration® by Inspiration Software, Inc.

After teachers have brainstormed and seen examples of essential questions and their usage with lessons, we continue to monitor the groups' work. At times, a group would comprehend and complete their work quickly. More often than not, this assignment would carry over as homework for groups that were struggling. Again, one-on-one work with individual groups was often important in assisting them with constructing an essential question before the next class. Occasionally, a group would come to class unhappy with the results. When that happened, they were advised that they would have time to tweak their question as they worked through The Web-Based Learning Model.

As you can see from the discussion and examples in this chapter, essential questions provide a starting point to begin giving students a chance to develop the higher-order thinking skills necessary for today's graduates.

Finding Your Way on the Web: A Guided Tour

"When you don't know where you're going, any road will do."
— ***Cheshire Cat***, *Alice in Wonderland*

Many potentially great ideas for lesson plans that integrate technology go awry because the ideas seem to require too much technical skill of the person trying to create them or use them. That doesn't have to be the case. Many teachers have learned the technical skills necessary to develop engaging online student-based activities.

A **Guided Tour** is a Web-based student activity that is a collection of Web sites. The teacher puts the collected links into a document. The student is guided through the Web sites by questions that ask for specific information. Since that is the case, it seems that the natural place to start would be in front of the computer.

Like any good lesson plan, pre-planning is essential to the success of your project. Let us suppose that a team of seventh-grade middle school teachers—including a language arts, science, and math teacher—decide they want to do an interdisciplinary unit on a topic that would be of interest and relevance to their students. That should be a realistic goal. In order to be successful, the teachers would need to plan the approach they would take. The project is more likely to fail because of a lack of planning, not because of a lack of technical skill. We need to remember that simple fact.

Often the technology makes us forget that great lessons come from great planning. Nevertheless, a unit that integrates technology, like any other unit, needs to be planned through brainstorming, developing essential questions, and aligning teaching to the appropriate standards. Only after these vital components of lesson development have occurred should teachers begin to tackle the technical aspects of a unit.

It is virtually impossible to develop good instructional material by going directly to the Web and performing random searches. There must be some structure and a sense of purpose from the start. For the technology novice or for the experienced teacher who wishes to tightly control student access to Web sites, creating a Guided Tour is an easy way to begin.

We are concerned about how we can protect students from getting into trouble on the Web. Unsupervised students using computers can be a nightmare for teachers. Teachers concerns are valid. Acceptable use policies and finely honed classroom management skills will lessen the problem. However, as with any classroom problem, the solution rests with a well-developed lesson plan that focuses and directs students as they investigate and explore a unit of study. As effective teachers, we cannot rely on students finding their own way in a lesson. Rather, we must design courses with specific learning goals and objectives in mind that go through final assessment. Teachers can find ways to make the act of learning compelling and directed for students.

One of the first steps in The Web-Based Learning Model is creating a Guided Tour. The Guided Tour evens the playing field for students. Whether or not the student has had access to computers or to the Web, the activity allows all students to experience success and complete an Internet project. Excellent for introducing students to the Web, the Guided Tour is structured so teachers can monitor the search for information by limiting the Web sites that students may investigate.

Guided Tours are one of the most frequently used Web-based activities because they are excellent for review, can be developed quickly, and fit well within a class period. (Most other Web-based activities require longer periods of time to complete.) Another reason for the popularity of Guided Tours is that they can be shared within the learning community.

Process Step 1: Guided Tour

In developing a Guided Tour, the teacher focuses on what a student needs to know and be able to do upon completing the unit of study. Having focused on the essential question, the teacher selects a topic and researches Web links that relate to the topic. The teacher creates a hotlist and questions centered upon the instructional theme. As mentioned earlier, the term *hotlist* refers to a collection of Web site addresses (URLs) that match a particular topic or concept.

Each link within a hotlist is annotated, giving the user a summary that describes the site; this is key to making a hotlist useable. The brief description of what information is found at that Web site allows the teacher to use the list over a period of time. While the initial list may contain only a few sites, over time the list may grow and may be used for other activities. A hotlist entry may be as brief as:

Cost of Living Analysis

<http://www.datamasters.com/cgi-bin/col.pl>. *This site contains information on the cost of relocating from one state/city to another state/city.*

As time passes, we tend to forget what was at a particular site. The entry example provides just enough information so that several weeks or months later a person would know what information was available at the Web site.

As mentioned earlier, a Guided Tour is excellent for beginning technology users since it requires basic skills (copy and paste) for the creator and only navigation skills for the user.

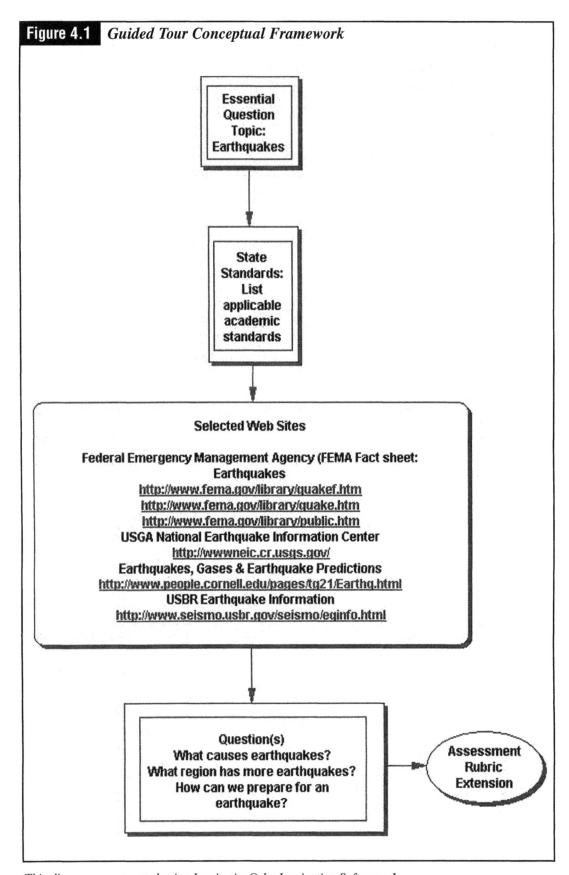

Figure 4.1 *Guided Tour Conceptual Framework*

Essential
Question
Topic:
Earthquakes

State
Standards:
List
applicable
academic
standards

Selected Web Sites

Federal Emergency Management Agency (FEMA Fact sheet:
Earthquakes
http://www.fema.gov/library/quakef.htm
http://www.fema.gov/library/quake.htm
http://www.fema.gov/library/public.htm
USGA National Earthquake Information Center
http://wwwneic.cr.usgs.gov/
Earthquakes, Gases & Earthquake Predictions
http://www.people.cornell.edu/pages/tg21/Earthq.html
USBR Earthquake Information
http://www.seismo.usbr.gov/seismo/eginfo.html

Question(s)
What causes earthquakes?
What region has more earthquakes?
How can we prepare for an
earthquake?

Assessment
Rubric
Extension

This diagram was created using Inspiration® by Inspiration Software, Inc.

Guided Tour Conceptual Framework

The Guided Tour Template separates the key areas that a Guided Tour should have in order to be effective. For instance:

First, the topic and the essential question should be defined. While it is very easy to skip over framing an essential question, to do so limits the use of the Guided Tour. If we are focusing on the larger issues, as we do when we define the essential question, it is an easier path to building the Guided Tour into a more demanding Web-based learning model. Consider the example essential question dealing with waste and recycling in the previous chapter. Once the question was defined, the teacher could then proceed with collecting Web sites and developing questions. In time, this activity could be adapted to a CyberInquiry or WebQuest. *(See Figure 4.2.)*

Figure 4.2 | *Recycling Waste Guided Tour by Doug Purinton, Broome High School*

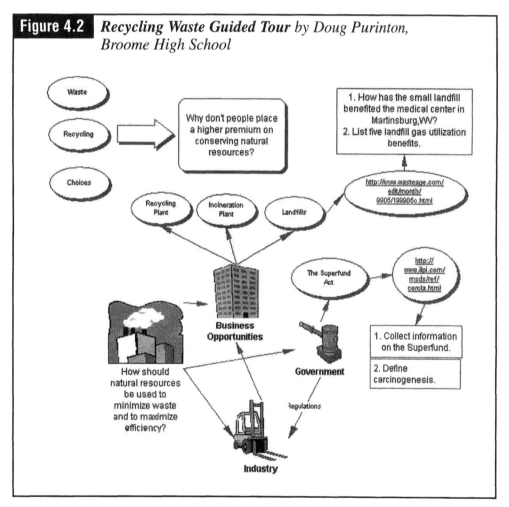

This diagram was created using Inspiration® by Inspiration Software, Inc.

Second, the academic standards that are being targeted by this instruction are listed. By listing the academic standards, both the teacher and the student remain focused on what the student needs to know and do.

Third, the teacher collects Web sites that will guide the student in the learning.

Fourth, the teacher asks leading questions that may be answered after viewing the designated Web sites.

Fifth, the teacher creates a rubric to guide the assessment of the student groups.

The actual skills required in creating a Guided Tour focus on five technical areas: learning to search, creating a hotlist, creating a Guided Tour, creating an HTML file, and posting a Web page.

Skill 1: Learn to Search

Gathering information effectively and efficiently is a necessary skill. If we do not learn to access the information available through the Web efficiently, we will find ourselves wandering aimlessly around the Web. Learning to search provides teachers efficient access to the vast amount of information available on the Internet. To begin your search:

- **Select a search engine.** When teaching teachers to search, first try a filtered search engine such as Yahooligans! **<http://www.yahooligans. com/>** or Searchopolis **<http://www.searchopolis.com/>**. A filtered search engine screens material that is offensive to children and/or families. Although filtered search engines do not guarantee that the sites are wholesome, educational, and appropriate, they do provide a safeguard. It is important that teachers experiment and see what information comes up on a filtered search engine and on a search engine that is unfiltered (e.g., Google **<http://www.google.com/>**, Yahoo! **<http://www.yahoo.com/>**, or Alta Vista **<http://www.altavista.com/>**).

- **Practice the search for information.** One of the most critical skills in locating information on the Web is narrowing the topic sufficiently to limit the list of sites. One way to develop any skill is to practice. Worksheets that require teachers to search for a wide range of information are one quick way to develop the skill. Awarding prizes to the teacher who completes the worksheet quickly and accurately makes the search fun. A sample worksheet can be developed that asks questions or requests information such as:

1. Where was Millard Fillmore born?
2. Print or show me a recipe for chocolate chip cookies.
3. Locate a picture of Monticello. Print or show me.
4. Where is 06712?
5. What is the Web address for a site that would give students writing tips from Judy Blume?

Before introducing Internet projects to students, the teacher must be familiar enough with search engines to use them correctly.

Skill 2: Create a Hotlist

A hotlist is a collection of Internet sites on one topic. Collecting hotlists is a necessary step before creating a Guided Tour, a CyberInquiry, or a WebQuest. The teacher may create a hotlist. To be useful, hotlists should include a brief statement about what is at the particular address. To be sure that the hotlists are accurate, teachers should use the **Copy** and **Paste** commands to enter Web site addresses into a word processing program (as explained in the last section of this chapter).

Skill 3: Create a Guided Tour

Saint Francis of Assisi tells us that we should "start by doing what's necessary, then do what's possible, and suddenly you are doing the impossible." Web-based learning is very much like that. The first time a teacher entertains the notion that lessons can be built with the Web is daunting. But after the first few tries, it becomes easier.

Guided Tours are excellent for a beginning Internet user because only basic technical skills are required. Introducing students to the Internet for the first time, a wise teacher will use a Guided Tour to assess student familiarity with the navigation skills necessary to use the Internet. Using a hotlist is an easy way for a teacher to begin practicing the skills necessary in creating a Guided Tour. Collections of Web sites that are annotated are available at Kathy Schrock's Web site for educators at **<http://school.discovery. com/schrockguide/>**.

As the topics are explored, a teacher may determine what students need to know about the topic, or may wonder how experienced the students are in using the Web. Do they all know navigation skills? What navigation skills need to be included in the Guided Tour (e.g., **Back, Print, Click**)? The reader may wish to refer to the Guided Tour Template on page 36. Note that the Guided Tour has an essential question, an annotated list of relevant sites, and questions that students must answer at these sites.

Skill 4: Create an HTML File

By creating a Web page, the teacher ensures that the Guided Tour may be used by an unlimited number of students and that all students, even those students who are not expert at using the Web, may participate. The Web page also ensures that students remain on task and do not wander around the Web. Since the Web addresses are linked directly, a student would need minimal skills (the ability to click on a link) to navigate a Guided Tour.

Skill 5: Post Your Web Page

The truly wondrous part of the Web is the vast amount of information that is available. The wealth of information—including countless lesson plans and ideas—would have taken an entire career to collect in times past. Now, it is a mouse click away—and it is something that we can share collegially when we post our plans and resources on the Web. By posting a Web page, we become part of a global community of educators.

The information and the skills learned in the Guided Tour lead to a Scavenger Hunt in which search skills are emphasized. In each step, however, the skills needed by the teacher become increasingly more complex. Additionally, if the teacher continues to work with one topic or theme, a very complex task, such as creating a WebQuest—which takes student thinking to the highest level—becomes more manageable for the teacher.

Organizing the Training

Several worksheets and templates can be used to guide the teacher during training. Following are sample worksheets, templates, and assignments that were developed as part of the professional development process.

Example 4.1 *Sample Worksheet*

Comparing and Evaluating Guided Tours

1. Navigate to **<http://www.spa3.k12.sc.us/Guided.html>** and scroll to the table at the bottom.

2. With your group, answer the following questions for each Guided Tour your group examined.

   ✓ What was the name of the Guided Tour? _____
   _____

   ✓ Did the Guided Tour have a clearly recognizable instructional topic?____
   _____

   ✓ Were lesson objectives provided? If so, were they clear to students and instructors?_____
   _____

   ✓ Was the Guided Tour aligned with state curriculum standards? _____
   _____

   ✓ Were the Web sites used in the Guided Tour useful in answering the questions? Were there any problems with the Web sites used? If so, what were they? How could such problems be addressed? _____
   _____

   ✓ Was a scoring rubric provided? Was it clear to students how they would be evaluated?_____
   _____

   ✓ Be prepared to explain to the class which aspects of each Guided Tour were most closely aligned with the conceptual framework and which aspects were least closely aligned with the conceptual framework._____
   _____

The purpose of the sample worksheet is to remind teachers of the characteristics of a well-developed Guided Tour. We then ask teachers to create their own Guided Tour using the template that follows.

Example 4.2   *Sample Template*

Guided Tour Template

Essential Question:
Concept: **Topic:**
Subject: Grade Level:

Curriculum Standards: What strands and topics are students going to be able to know and do after they study this material? Copy and paste standards from the State Department of Education site. (In South Carolina: **http://www.sde.state. sc.us/sde/test123/standard.htm**)

Annotated list of sites for students to explore: The number of sites may be as few as one or as many as four or five.

What are the **questions** that a student should answer at each site?

Is there an **extension or enrichment activity** for those students who finish the material quickly?

Assessment—Is there a rubric to determine assessment?
Are worksheets or other materials required for the assessment?

As part of the process leading to development of a Guided Tour, we ask the teacher to create a Guided Tour from the template shown in Example 4.2. The technology skills become necessary to create the tour; however, the emphasis of topic, extension, and assessment is done before the technology skill is emphasized. This keeps the teacher focused on the qualities necessary to develop a strong lesson.

Example 4.3 | *Sample Assignment*

Guided Tour Assignment

1. Take the lesson that you created earlier and determine the topic on which to create a Guided Tour.

2. In your template, list the academic standards topics and strands that a student should know and be able to do after the Guided Tour.

3. Open your browser and begin to search. Using search techniques you have learned, find sites that would provide information about the topic. For the purpose of this assignment, you must find a minimum of six sites and annotate them.

4. Open your word processor. As you find each site, copy and paste the URL into the word processor. Use the template design. Annotate the URL so you will know what information is available at the site. (Remember that if you do not use this site for this particular exercise, you may use it later for another assignment.)

5. Using your file management skills, save the annotated list in a folder that is named with the title of your Guided Tour.

6. Create a folder in which to bookmark all sites in your browser.

7. Frame questions for your students to answer at the sites that you decide to use. (You do not have to use all of your sites.) Type the questions that you would like students to answer into the template.

8. Determine the assessment that you will use to evaluate the student's work on the Guided Tour.

9. Save the template as a Web page.

10. If you like, add a background to the Web document and add graphics. (Remember that graphics must be saved to the same folder as the Web document to make it easier to post it on a Web server. Do not overdo it with the graphics!)

11. Congratulations! You have completed your first two class requirements: An annotated hotlist, and a Guided Tour! Make plans to post your work and to share with others.

Exhibit Center

From here, we shall present an annotated list of authentic examples of teacher-created activities for Guided Tours. (Chapters 5 through 9 also will include Exhibit Centers that feature work that is characteristic of the topics discussed.)

Guided Tours can be useful in teaching students the basics of navigating the Web. For the teacher, Guided Tours are good first-time activities for making hotlists and writing questions for an activity. Please note the range that the following examples of Guided Tours encompass. They vary widely from one another. The activities differ in terms of their complexity and thoroughness; however, notice how Guided Tours rely on questions characterized by lower levels of Bloom's Taxonomy. Rarely do the questions get to the level of Synthesis or Evaluation.

Exhibit 4.1 | *Understanding Volcanoes*

Understanding Volcanoes

http://www.spa3.k12.sc.us/Volcano.html

Student _____

1. Look at the menu items at the top of the page. Click once on Bookmarks. Click once on the folder "Volcanoes" **<http://volcano.und.nodak.edu/>**.
2. Click once on the Bookmark "Volcano World."
3. When the Volcano World home page opens, click once on "Teaching and Learning," which is located on the left side of the page.
4. Using the down arrow on the right side of the keyboard, scroll down the page until you see "Volcano Facts."
5. Click once on "Volcano Facts." Click once on "Blasts from the Past: Great Eruptions."

Click on "Toba, Indonesia."
1. What lakes were formed by glacial erosion? _____
2. What lakes were formed by down-dropping of large blocks of crust?

   _____
3. What kind of rocks surround Lake Toba? _____
4. How long did the volcanic eruption last? _____
5. Click once on Print, located on the toolbar.
6. Find BACK on the toolbar. Click it to go back to the home page of Volcano World.
7. Click on "Volcanoes of the World."
8. Click on the map of North America.
9. Click on California.

Exhibit 4.1 *Understanding Volcanoes* *(continued)*

10. Click on a volcano in California. Answer the following questions:
11. Where is it located? _____
12. What is its name?   _____
13. List three facts about the volcano.

    _____

    _____

    _____

14. Click Print on the toolbar.

Visit Cascades Volcano Observatory at
http://Vulcan.wr.usgs.gov/.

1. Click once on "Bookmarks." Click once on the Bookmark "Cascades Volcano Observatory."
2. Scientists predicted that Mount St. Helens might erupt by what year?

    _____
3. What year did Mount St. Helens erupt? _____
4. How many active volcanoes are there in the United States? _____
5. What Cascade Range volcano is the most likely to erupt next?

    _____
6. What causes airplanes and helicopters to be damaged by eruptions even many miles away? _____
7. Click once on the toolbar, "Print."

Commentary: There are several positive characteristics about the Guided Tour shown in Exhibit 4.1. For the student new to the Internet, directions for where and what to click are clearly explained. It is clear from the questioning, that the teacher closely examined the Web sites used in the activity and was able to generate very useful knowledge-based inquiries.

However, there are some obvious deficiencies with this activity. First, there are no objectives stated for the students to view. Even if the objectives are not listed on the activity, a link to the objectives should be provided. This Guided Tour also lacks an introduction to "hook" the students. The teacher may have set up the activity for the class before sending them to the computer, which makes a catchy introduction less vital. Finally, the teacher does not state how the students will be graded. There is no rubric or score guide. Again, if the expectations were clearly stated to the class beforehand, having a link to a rubric is not essential.

Exhibit 4.2 *Understanding Life Forms*

Understanding Life Forms

http://www.spa3.k12.sc.us/LifeForms.html

Student _____

1. Navigage to: **http://www.biology.about.com/science/
   biology/library/weekly/aa31600a.htm**.
2. When the "Journey into the Cell" page opens, scroll down to the table
   of information.
3. Answer the following questions:
   What are lysosomes?_____
   What does the Endoplasmic Reticulum do? _____
   What are Ribosomes?_____
4. Explore the page. Find out why the Web page was developed. If you
   find the information, print it.

**Visit Dictionary of Cell Biology at http://www.mblab.gla.ac.uk/ dic-
tionary/.** The dictionary is a search feature that is intended to provide
quick access to terms frequently encountered in biology.

1. Using the information that you printed on lysosomes, use the search
   feature to look up a term. What term did you search for?

   _____
2. Is the information here different from what you found at Journey into
   the Cells, or the same? How? _____
3. Find BACK on the toolbar. Click to go back to the home page of the
   Dictionary of Cell Biology.
4. Scroll down the page and click on "DNA."
5. How many hits did you receive on DNA? _____
6. How many records were there for DNA? _____

**Click on Bookmark. Visit Cell Basics. http://esg-www.mit.edu:8001/
esgbio/cb/cellbasics.html**

1. Print the page.
2. List three properties that a living thing must have.
3. List the two reasons that the cell is the fundamental unit of life.
4. What four elements make up almost the entire composition of all living organisms?

Commentary: This example is similar to Exhibit 4.1 in that it provides great
detail to the student new to navigating the Internet. The addition of clearly
defined objectives and grading criteria would make this Guided Tour more
useful for the student.

Exhibit 4.3 *Tessellations Guided Tour*

Tessellations Guided Tour

by Barbour Bordogna

http://www.spa3.k12.sc.us/GuidedTours/Tessellations/
TesselationsGT.htm

What is a tessellation?

What is M. C. Escher known for?

What kinds of meanings do you find in tessellations?

Why was The Palace at Alhambra important to Escher?

What did Escher want to be before he started tessellating?

Visit the site below to answer these questions and to begin learning about tessellations.

http://library.advanced.org/16661/escher.html

The following is an excerpt from the South Carolina Curriculum Standards (1998) for Third Grade Mathematics.

Geometry and Spatial Sense

Explore informally tessellations, symmetry, congruence, similarity, scale, perspective, angles, and networks.

The student will use manipulatives to create tessellations.

Commentary: This Guided Tour provides much less detail than the previous two exhibits, but it does display one important feature: The teacher provides a description of the target objectives. This example would not be suitable for the novice to the Internet. The teacher does not provide step-by-step instructions to students on how to navigate to the Web site or what exactly to look for when they arrive there. Also, as in the previous examples, the students will not know how they will be graded unless the teachers has explained in class how the activity will be evaluated.

Exhibit 4.4 *Anne Frank and the Children of the Holocaust*

Anne Frank and the Children of the Holocaust

Adapted from a WebQuest by Jim Heffner, Polly Hembree, and Alicia Womick

Over one million children under the age of sixteen died in the Holocaust. Anne Frank was one of them.

http://www.spa3.k12.sc.us/GuidedTours/annefrank/frank.html

Objective: The student will be able to better understand the courage and heroic spirit of Anne Frank and other children of the Holocaust.

Materials: paper, pencil, and Internet

Introduction: As we begin our study of World War II, we will take time to learn about one of the most unlikely heroes of the 20th century. Anne Frank was a child of the Holocaust who kept a diary that chronicled her years in hiding from Nazi soldiers.

Read the literature about the children of the Holocaust. Select works that especially express the courage and heroic spirit of the children. Answer the questions under each link.

Anne Frank's Diary... Selected Entries
http://www.annefrank.com/
Why did Anne Frank think that Jews were being murdered in 1942?
What were German college students required to do in 1943? What happened if they didn't?
What evidence is there that Anne was receiving news about the war even while she and her family were in hiding?
What was Anne's outlook like by February 1943?

Exhibit 4.4 **Anne Frank and the Children of the Holocaust** *(continued)*

Stories of Survivors
http://spidey.sfusd.k12.ca.us/schwww/sch773/review/ngo.html
In which country did Lida Mordehay live?
What was the yellow star? Who had to wear it?
Why didn't Lida and her brother wear the yellow star?
What were concentration camps?
How many Jews does Lida state were murdered by the Germans? Is this
     number accurate?

Commentary: As is clear from this example, Guided Tours need not focus exclusively on searching for dry facts. Guided Tours may be opportunities for students to explore emotional, sensitive information and to have time to reflect about what they have discovered. While some would call the previous example a WebQuest, we reserve that term for a Web-based activity that requires a student to synthesize, evaluate, and transform the information. This activity lacks that higher-order activity. In addition, this activity lacks the cognitive dissonance that a well-developed WebQuest has.

Exhibit 4.5 *Salaries and Professional Basketball Players*

Salaries and Professional Basketball Players

Complete Hotlist and Guided Tour by Robin Breitenbach, Pam Cook, and Ann Hudson

http://www.spa3.k12.sc.us/WebQuests/Basketball/bballhotlist.htm

Hotlist
http://tcrcc.com/cost.htm
Cost of living in South Carolina with other comparisons.

http://www.datamasters.com/cgi-bin/col.pl
Cost of relocation from one state/city to another state/city based on salary.

http://www.datamasters.com/survey.html
Salary comparisons in the computer industry by region.

http://www2.hpe.com/hpedc/cost.html
Cost of Living for High Point, NC w/ Comparisons to Other North Carolina cities.

Exhibit 4.5 *Salaries and Professional Basketball Players (continued)*

http://www.infoplease.com/ipa/a0763363.html
Study of national housing costs

http://www.jgstarlink.com/wealthcare/profath.htm
Insurance for professional athletes

http://www.aha-ins.com/college_pro_draft.htm
Professional athlete's career-ending disability

http://www.stonehopper.com/atw/pp/pro.html
Cost of injury for professional athletes

http://collegian.ksu.edu/issues/v101/su/n166/sports/sports-salaries-sam.html
Professional athletes deserve high salaries.

http://www3.nando.net/newsroom/ap/bkb/1995/nba/cha/feat/archive/112995/cha36531.html
Hornets sign six-year deal to play in Charlotte coliseum.

http://www.buildeval.com/dataindex.html
Cost of building a variety of different structures

http://www.sonic.net/elmolino/paper/dec1898/salaries.shtml
Argument for high player salaries

http://www.alligator.org/edit/issues/96-sumr/960723/c01col.htm
Columnist opposes NBA salaries.

http://www.members.home.net/lmcoon/salarycap.htm
Complete information about salary cap

http://nationalcounseling.com/timeout.html
Crisis in professional sports (violence and high salaries)

http://www.oregonlive.com/todaysnews/9806/st063004.html
NBA lockout effect on fans

http://abcnews.go.com/sections/business/dailynews/ nbas-trike981221.html
Effect of lockout on municipalities

http://fl.mlive.com/pistons/stories/19981113qanda.html
Question-and-answer with David Stern, NBA commissioner

http://abcnews.go.com/sections/business/DailyNews/ nbare-turn990106.html
Economic impact of NBA season on local business.

http://www.oregonlive.com/todaysnews/9806/st063015.html
NBA lockout facts

http://www.reporternews.com/sports/candy1019.html
Vehement disagreement of players earning high salaries

Exhibit 4.5 *Salaries and Professional Basketball Players (continued)*

http://www.piu.org/products.htm
Insurance underwriter for professional athletes

The hotlist does not necessarily need to be shared directly with the students, but for the teacher it becomes an invaluable resource. When looking back on this hotlist a year from now, the teacher would have little trouble browsing through this list and identifying the contents for a particular Web site. The hotlist will also become a cornerstone for the remaining activities in the framework. By developing a thorough, annotated hotlist at the beginning, the teacher will have plenty of sites to work with when developing a WebQuest at a later date.

Salaries and Professional Basketball Players Guided Tour
**http://www.spa3.k12.sc.us/WebQuests/Basketball/
MathGuidedTour2.htm**

- Why do professional athletes make so much money?
- How can we look at players' salaries in terms of percentages?
- How do your choices as a consumer influence players' salaries?

By completing this Guided Tour, you will be able to explain how a market economy drives up salaries that professional sports players earn.

You will be able to compare the percentage of increase/decrease in players' salaries among three professional sports. Use the Web site link provided to find the information needed to answer the following questions. Remember, read carefully.
http://collegian.ksu.edu/issues/v101/su/n166/sports/sports-salaries-sam.html

1. How does consumer demand drive up the salaries of professional athletes?
2. Compare Brett Favre's salary to that of a professional who makes $40,000 a year. What percent more does Favre make?
3. What percent more does Favre make than Rodriquez? How about Maddux?
4. What are some possible reasons for these differences?
5. Other than market forces, what other factors could justify paying professional athletes such high salaries?

As with all projects, we encourage teachers to develop rubrics to guide student assessment. Expected performance should be stated.

Exhibit 4.5 *Salaries and Professional Basketball Players (continued)*

Evaluation

	Inadequate	Adequate	Good	Superior
Content	Answers show evidence of little or no information collected from research.	Answers show incomplete or inaccurate information collected from research.	Answers show accurate and adequate information collected from research.	Answers show accurate and abundant information collected from research.
Conventions	Answers are not presented in complete sentence form, or are in sentence form with major problems in mechanics.	Many answers are not presented in complete sentence form, or are in sentence form with major problems in mechanics.	Answers are in sentence form but contain minor problems in mechanics.	Answers are in sentence form with little or no problems in mechanics.

Rubric for Data Collection Basketball Salaries

Commentary: This Guided Tour meets all of the requirements of fully developed activity. At the beginning, the teacher tells the students exactly what they will learn and accomplish by completing this activity. Leading questions help to introduce the activity and to prepare students for the detailed questions that lie ahead. The directions do not lead the student step-by-step, but the depth and number of questions do not make such detailed instructions essential.

Exhibit 4.6 *Guided Tour–Astronauts*

Guided Tour—Astronauts

http://www.spa3.k12.sc.us/GuidedTours/astronauts/AstronautGT.htm

John Glenn became the oldest person to travel into space. To begin to acquire some background as well as to learn about the effects of space on the human body, complete this Guided Tour.

Objectives:

- ■ Students will be able to explain the preparation astronauts must undergo before traveling in space.
- ■ Students will analyze the significance of John Glenn's most recent space voyage.

Instructions: Please navigate to the following Web site:

http://spacelink.nasa.gov/NASA.Projects/Human.Exploration. and.Development.of.Space/Human.Space.Flight/Shuttle/Shuttle. Missions/Flight.092.STS-95/John.Glenn.Returns.to.Space/

Answer the questions below. Please type your answers on a Word document.

1. Describe the preparation an astronaut must undergo before making a flight into space.
2. Why was John Glenn's initial voyage into space such a significant event?
3. What is the significance of Glenn's most recent trip on the space shuttle?
4. What are some of the risks astronauts accept when traveling in space?

After you have completed your answers, use the Discovery form to present the material to the class.

Commentary: This Guided Tour identifies learning objectives, provides clear instructions, and uses specific questions. This activity does not provide a link to academic standards or a grading rubric. There also is an extension activity. Note that the instructions direct students to use a Discovery form to present information to the class. In Chapter 7, Internet Discoveries will be explained further.

Exhibit 4.7 *Inventions*

Inventions

http://www.spa3.k12.sc.us/Inventions.htm

Would you like to read about some famous inventions? How about seeing some inventions created by other students? Would you like to make your own invention?

Visit the following invention links:

Henry Ford Museum & Greenfield Village Online Histories
http://www.hfmgv.org/histories/index.html
Click on "Stories of Inventors" link.

Ben Franklin's: Glimpses of the Man
http://sln.fi.edu/franklin/rotten.html
Read information at the "Inventor" link.

About.com Kid Inventions Page
http://inventors.miningco.com/science/inventors/cs/kidinventions/
index.htm

3-M Collaborative Invention Unit Page
http://mustang.coled.umn.edu/inventing/inventing.html

Can you tell me what the four steps are to being an inventor?

Would you like to check up on how much you learned at these Web sites? Complete an Inventor Worksheet.

Inventor Worksheet

What did each of these people invent? (Look at Henry Ford Museum at **http://www.hfmgv.org/histories/**.)
■ Henry Ford
■ The Wright Brothers
■ Thomas Edison

Were they inventors when they were children?

Exhibit 4.7 *Inventions (continued)*

Describe what each of these inventors did as children that might have been unusual.

- Henry Ford
- The Wright Brothers
- Thomas Edison

Go to the Kid's Inventions Page at **http://inventors.miningco.com/ science/inventors/cs/kidinventions/index.htm**.

Answer these questions:

- What invention is the most useful? Why?
- Which invention looks like the hardest to use?
- Which invention looks like the most fun to use?
- To find out the steps that you need to take to make your own invention look at the 3-M page again at **http://mustang.coled.umn.edu/ inventing/inventing.html**.

Look around your home or your school. What ideas do you have for inventions that would make your life easier?

Extension Activity for Invention Guided Tour

- Choose one of your ideas to invent.
- What materials would you need?
- Draw some sketches of your invention. Show them to your parents or to your teacher.

Commentary: This is an engaging activity. Although the learning objectives and academic standards are not explicitly stated, students have an opportunity to do some creative thinking on the activity extension. Note that even though Guided Tours are introductory in nature, they can be imaginative and challenging.

Exhibit 4.8 *The 1960s–The Vietnam War*

The 1960s—The Vietnam War

http://www.spa3.k12.sc.us/guidedtours/vietnam/vietnamwar.htm

Objectives:
- Students will read and analyze information about the Vietnam War and the MIA (Missing in Action) issue.
- Students will display an understanding of material by writing a short essay advising the President on current foreign policy.

State Academic Standards:

II. Power, Authority and Governance: Government/Political Science

12.6.3 Analyze how U.S. foreign policy is formulated and the means by which it is carried out.

Introduction: Throughout the 1960s and early 1970s, the United States military was involved in a massive military conflict in Vietnam in Southeast Asia. The war inflicted terrible hardships on both Vietnamese and American people alike. One of the most painful chapters of the war has been the search for American soldiers who were classified as Missing in Action (MIA) at the end of the war. To this day, some American families and politicians still suspect that the Vietnamese government has withheld information regarding the whereabouts and status of hundreds of American soldiers believed to be MIA.

Instructions: Please take a look at the Web site **http://www.pbs.org/wgbh/amex/vietnam/trenches/mia.html**. When you finish reading at the site, answer the following questions and begin working on the extension activity. Answers will be graded based on the Internet Activity rubric handed out at the beginning of the year.

Questions:

What was Operation Homecoming?

What is the official stance of the U.S. and Vietnamese governments on American MIAs?

Of those Americans held prisoner by Vietnam, what was their primary role in the war?

Describe the treatment of American prisoners of war by the Vietnamese army.

How did American prisoners of war "confound" their captors?

Exhibit 4.8 *The 1960s–The Vietnam War* (continued)

How did Americans at home attempt to improve conditions for prisoners of war?

What did United Nations worker, Ted Schweitzer, discover in the Central Military Museum in Hanoi in 1989?

Extension: In light of the MIA debate, if you were asked to advise the U.S. president on foreign relations, what would be your advice concerning relations with Vietnam?

Commentary: This Guided Tour stands out from the others in one major respect: It is a small part of what would most likely be a larger unit. The title of the activity indicates the decade—the 1960s—and also a specific event—the Vietnam War. In a broad instructional unit like teaching the 1960s, a teacher may create a half-dozen different Guided Tours to begin building background knowledge for students.

Technical Corner

For technical assistance with the topics discussed in this chapter, please refer to the Appendix.

Skill	Description	Appendix Page Number
Chapter 4 Technical Corner		
Copying and Pasting Between Programs	Allows user to copy Web site URL and paste it into a word processor or Web page editor.	181
File and Bookmark Management	Details importance of maintaining organized system of files and Internet sites in creating Web-based learning activities. Demonstrates saving, naming, and creating files and folders.	183

Lost in Space: A Scavenger Hunt

"Nothing is exciting if you know what the outcome is going to be."
— Joseph Campbell

Do you remember the first time you went on a scavenger hunt? A traditional staple of parties, scavenger hunts provide groups of people with a task to complete. Whether the scavenger hunt involves collecting artifacts—such as a school yearbook or a particular kind of shoe—or calls for following directions to a treasure chest, most people enjoy the activity.

How do we go about creating a **Scavenger Hunt** as one of the six process steps in The Web-Based Learning Model? As we design a Scavenger Hunt, it is important that we design it so that individuals must work together to achieve success. The task should be sufficiently complicated so that it can be separated into various skills. This allows each group member to contribute—that is important.

Web-based Scavenger Hunts enjoy all of the same qualities of the more traditional scavenger hunt and make an excellent activity for getting students excited about using technology for learning. In Chapter 4, we introduced the development of a Guided Tour dealing with professional athletes, which was created by a team of middle school teachers. The teacher team desired to create a fully integrated technology unit that eventually would lead to a WebQuest. Part of working in the Web-based learning framework led them to develop a Scavenger Hunt.

Unlike the Guided Tour where the teacher pre-selects the Web sites and limits the content that students explore through closely determined questions, the Scavenger Hunt is a blank template. Even if the teacher pre-selects certain Web sites for younger students to visit, the teacher leaves the search broad enough that students can manipulate the Web site to generate questions and then manipulate the information to make a report to the class and the teacher.

For the older student, however, the teacher goes a step further. Rather than pre-selecting material for the students to search, the teacher provides background material (perhaps through the Guided Tour or through a topic introduction) on the topic that the class will explore. The background information is important. Students must know enough about the topic so that they will know how to begin their search. A key component of the Scavenger Hunt is that students brainstorm ideas in learning groups and develop keywords and a strategy on how to conduct the search for information. After they have completed this preliminary work, they begin to use and manipulate the information for which they have searched.

Process Step 2: Scavenger Hunt

The Scavenger Hunt is more involved than the Guided Tour and requires higher technical skills for the students. In order to complete a Scavenger Hunt, the students need to know how to formulate an effective search, how to copy and paste, and how to summarize what they have learned. As with all process steps, the steps may be combined in one lesson. A teacher may have a less technically advanced group of students completing a Guided Tour assignment while another group of students with more technical savvy are completing a Scavenger Hunt on the same topic.

In order to use the Scavenger Hunt with students, teachers first need to be well versed in how to effectively use a search engine to locate information on the Web. If a teacher does not know how to search or has never experienced the common problems in searching, it would be impossible for that instructor to teach students how to do it.

To design a Scavenger Hunt, a teacher constructs question(s) that relate to a topic being studied. If the teacher has collected links on the topic previously, the student could investigate the sites for interesting questions to use in a Scavenger Hunt. On the other hand, if the teacher were trying to find links for a Guided Tour, the student would enter a query about the subject in several search engines.

Scavenger Hunts can be of two primary types:
1. The teacher develops a series of questions on a topic, and a search engine or directory is used to locate the information.
2. The student develops a series of questions, and the teacher provides a hypertext link to a Web site where information can be found on the topic.

The model for the Scavenger Hunt is very similar to a Guided Tour. As discussed in Chapter 4, the Guided Tour begins with a broad topic that is being studied. An essential question is framed, and the concept that will be used to explore the essential question is stated. Finally, the academic standards the students are expected to know and be able to do are stated. The student then takes that information and writes several questions that he or she may wish to explore about the concept. Next, the student searches the Web, using the search template, to find sites where the answers to the questions may be found. Finally, a joint decision between the student and the teacher determines what final product the student will develop as a result of the information. The product may be a Guided Tour that will introduce other students to the topic, a Web page *(see Chapter 6)*, a PowerPoint show, or a research summary.

Several key concepts about Scavenger Hunts are important for the teacher to understand before setting students loose with the activity.

1. The student must be old enough to be able to evaluate information found at a Web site. Teachers of younger students may wish to provide the Web sites that the students explore to create their questions.
2. The student must have a basic understanding of the topic to be researched. The Scavenger Hunt should follow an introduction of the material that the student will research. This may be done through the traditional overview or through a Guided Tour.
3. The teacher creates the topic, essential question, concept, exploration, and standards connection for the student to guide the search.
4. The student creates the additional questions to be researched about the stated topic and concept.
5. The teacher monitors the student search, through a Web search template or through observation, to ensure that students stay on task and are skilled enough to focus their search.

Scavenger Hunt Conceptual Framework

The Scavenger Hunt conceptual framework looks similar to that of a Guided Tour. The primary difference is that in the Guided Tour, there are predetermined Web sites to visit with questions. In a Scavenger Hunt, the sites are not predetermined; instead, there is a predetermined topic.

Figure 5.1 *Scavenger Hunt Template*

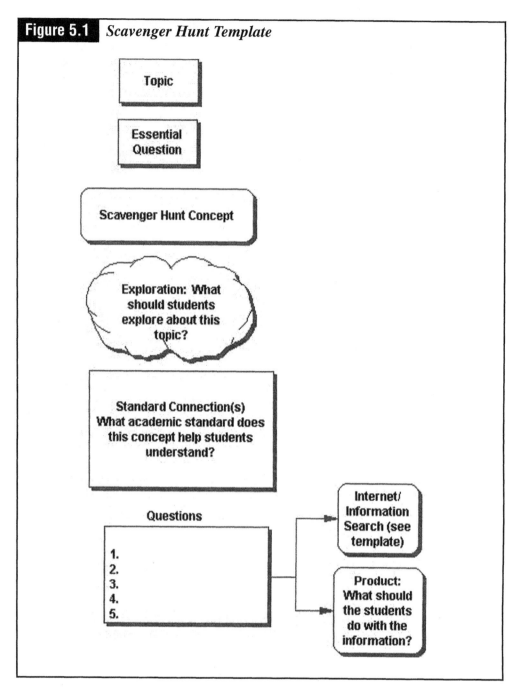

This diagram was created using Inspiration® by Inspiration Software, Inc.

Figure 5.2 *Completed Scavenger Hunt Template*

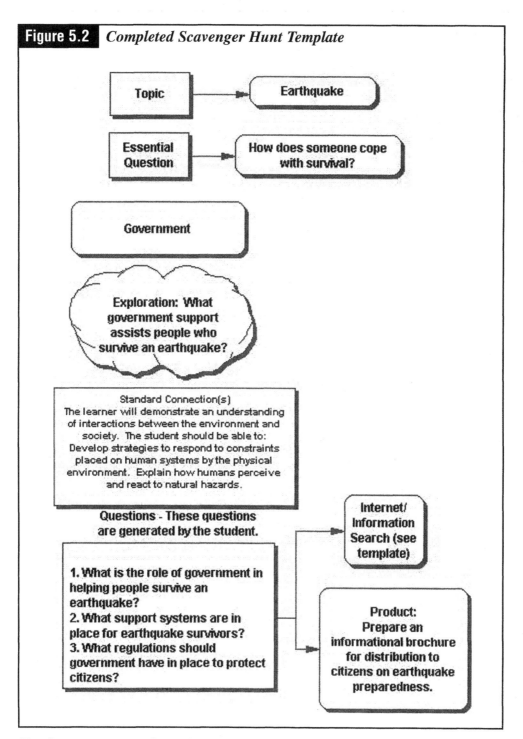

This diagram was created using Inspiration® by Inspiration Software, Inc.

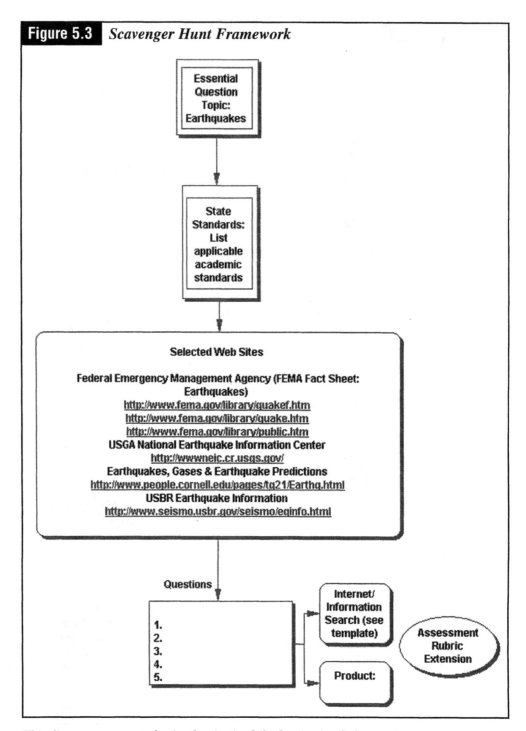

| Figure 5.3 | *Scavenger Hunt Framework* |

Essential Question Topic: Earthquakes

State Standards: List applicable academic standards

Selected Web Sites

Federal Emergency Management Agency (FEMA Fact Sheet: Earthquakes)
http://www.fema.gov/library/quakef.htm
http://www.fema.gov/library/quake.htm
http://www.fema.gov/library/public.htm
USGA National Earthquake Information Center
http://wwwneic.cr.usgs.gov/
Earthquakes, Gases & Earthquake Predictions
http://www.people.cornell.edu/pages/tg21/Earthq.html
USBR Earthquake Information
http://www.seismo.usbr.gov/seismo/eqinfo.html

Questions

1.
2.
3.
4.
5.

Internet/ Information Search (see template)

Assessment Rubric Extension

Product:

This diagram was created using Inspiration® by Inspiration Software, Inc.

Using a Search Template

One method for monitoring student searches is using a search template. The template directs the student in his or her search and allows the teacher to keep the focus on the instructional topic. Students are not allowed to wander without direction. Tips for teachers who are working with the template are as follows:

- When using the Scavenger Hunt template, a specific topic related to the current instructional unit is identified.
- The fill-in blank next to Search Engine is completed. Teachers may wish to steer students to Magellan **<http://magellan.excite.com/>** (green-light sites) or to Yahooligans! **<http://www.yahooligans.com/>** to limit access to inappropriate sites.
- Students brainstorm possible keywords to use in finding information on the topic. This should be a group activity.
- The keyword section is completed before getting on the Web. This activity should be done by a group of students. Students learn that they must be specific in order to find information efficiently on the Web.
- After the teacher approves, the student begins the search.

The purpose of tracking the sites visited is to help the student refine his or her search. If the student is unsuccessful, the teacher looks over the information and redirects the student.

Using the Scavenger Hunt Template example on page 60, students may evaluate information and do some analyses.

Scavenger Hunt Template

Name of topic to be researched:

Search Engine _____

Keyword(s) or phrase(s) used to conduct search:

1_____
2_____
3_____
4_____
5_____

1. Address and brief description of site visited:
URL: _____
Link (name): _____
Link (name): _____
Successful? Yes_____   No_____

2. Address and brief description of site visited:
URL: _____
Link (name): _____
Link (name): _____
Successful? Yes_____   No_____

3. Address and brief description of URL visited:
URL: _____
Link (name): _____
Link (name): _____
Successful? Yes_____   No_____

What else did you find that you might wish to pursue at another time?

_____
_____
_____
_____
_____

Student Teamwork

Student teamwork and collaboration is essential in using a Scavenger Hunt activity effectively. By carefully grouping students, teachers ensure that more experienced Web users are paired with less experienced users. Since the focus of the Scavenger Hunt is on gathering, evaluating, and reacting to information, all students can contribute to the activity even if a student has minimal experience with technology.

To ensure effective and successful student teamwork:

First, the teacher must be sure that the content to be researched is identified and that a rubric (criteria for mastery) defines the targeted learning.

Second, the teacher assigns students to groups by evaluating the skills and the abilities of each team member individually. Random assignments may result in teams that do not have the skills necessary to complete the activity successfully.

Third, the teacher arranges the classroom to facilitate the group interaction. Ideally, in a classroom, computers can be clustered. Even if the teacher has a one-computer classroom, the computer can be placed in a corner with a seating area to encourage brainstorming and discussion.

Fourth, group processes are taught. The role of each group member is discussed. What is the responsibility of the Web navigator? What should the recorder do? What are the responsibilities of the reporter?

Fifth, the teacher outlines a clear time line for the activities and establishes expectations for how the group will report its work.

Sixth, the objectives for the learning are clearly stated to the learners.

Seventh, the teacher continuously monitors the work of the group. Evaluation is based on observations of student performance or the criteria for mastery outlined in the rubric. By structuring the experience so group and individual evaluation is a part of the cooperative learning experience, students realize that what each of them does individually affects the work and success of the others. The teacher structures the work so students must share information.

Directions for Working in Groups

The motto of your group is "All for One, One for All." The motto means that in order to be successful each member of the group must accomplish his or her task successfully. You will be evaluated by fellow group members on your contribution to the group and will be evaluated by your teacher on how successfully you completed your individual task. The teacher will evaluate your group's work as well.

To be successful, you must follow these instructions:

■ Each group member should contribute ideas. Since each group member has a special skill, the information that is provided will be necessary to complete the group's task.

- Each group member must listen carefully to others' ideas.
- Everyone must be given a chance to speak.
- The teacher should be consulted only after each team member has had the opportunity to solve the problem.
- Everyone must agree with the report that is presented to the class. Each team member should initial the report before turning it in to the teacher.

After the teacher provides the directions to each student for working in a group, the teacher may wish to go ahead and assign roles. As students become familiar with their own special skills and abilities within the group process, students may select their own roles. A teacher would hand out the role descriptions to the students, review them with the students, and then answer any questions before leaving the group members to begin their initial group process.

The Roles

(These are sample roles for a Scavenger Hunt. Other roles may be developed as well.):

- *Web Navigator:* The Web navigator conducts the actual search for information that is found in the task.
  - Skills Required: The Web Navigator must be able to use the computer keyboard to type in information. The Navigator should be able to use search engines and directories to access information quickly. The Navigator must also know how to click on hypertext links, navigate on the Web, and type in addresses in the browser.
- *Reporter:* The Reporter is the group member responsible for reporting the key elements of the search to the entire group.
  - Skills Required: The Reporter must be comfortable with presenting ideas to the whole group in a clear, concise way. In addition to public speaking, the Reporter must be able to sift through information and determine the key points that must be incorporated into the presentation.
- *Recorder:* The Recorder is the group member responsible for recording the addresses of the Web sites visited and for summarizing the main ideas at each Web site.
  - Skills Required: The Recorder must be able to copy information accurately from the Web. The Recorder should read the information that is printed and outline information that may be important.
- *Organizer:* The Organizer is the person responsible for keeping all group members on task. The Organizer will also evaluate information that is collected. Finally, the Organizer will locate additional materials that may be in the school media center.
  - Skills Required: The Organizer must be able to use a card catalogue or to search the media center's reference collection. The Organizer must be able to establish a time line and keep all group members on task.

Teacher Collaboration

It is important that media specialists or teachers teach Web-searching skills. Even those students who are adept at using the Web may not understand how to focus the search. Just as a teacher would never think to assign a student a research paper without first reviewing how to search for appropriate resources, teachers should never assign a Scavenger Hunt without first reviewing the skills necessary. We encourage teachers and media specialists to collaborate in teaching these skills. The media specialist is the resident expert on reference materials. In addition, the media specialist is the expert on copyright laws and regulations. The time to address copyright issues is before research begins.

How can media specialists assist teachers as they learn to use search engines effectively? By focusing on one search engine, teachers are able to gain confidence and competence quickly. The key word is *one*. Select a search engine such as Google, **<http://www.google.com>**, which is very teacher-friendly, or limit your search to the Kathy Schrock directory at **<http://school.discovery.com/schrockguide/>**, which is subject-specific and annotated.

Once a teacher is comfortable using one search engine, the skill can be applied to other search engines or directories. The ability to access information may be one of the most important skills of the 21st century. It is a skill needed by the teacher and by the student. The unbelievable amount of information—of varying quality—available on the Web is staggering.

The number of returns (number of sites) that a student or teacher gets when searching for information and the relevance of the sites (whether they have anything to do with what we are looking for) may be frustrating. However, going to the Help menu or the advanced options of a search engine will assist in limiting the number of returns on a topic. Web sites that teach searching skills also are available.

To assist with a student's search, media specialists or teachers may discuss how to determine which hits to look at and explore. Students will often take the first one or two hits as the place to begin to research information. Emphasizing the importance of using critical thinking when searching the Web is of utmost importance. Students need to be critical consumers of Web information.

More often than not, students will pick up on this skill quickly—usually within one class period—and be ready to engage in meaningful and fruitful searches for information. If a computer lab is available, teachers may wish to teach search skills in that setting. The advantage of using the lab is that the teacher is better able to assess the skill level of each student. This basic information allows the teacher to better determine how to assign students to the cooperative learning group.

The instruction on searching focuses on the Scavenger Hunt Template. Prior to students sitting down at the computers, the teacher reviews what they will be doing. Questioning students about what strategy they would use to search for information will focus the purpose of the lesson.

The teacher may also determine whether or not students will need to be taught how to copy and paste the URLs they find to a Word document. If the teacher determines that the students need the additional instruction, the teacher may team with the media specialist or the school technology teacher to deliver these technical skills.

An important part of the lesson would be to teach students to annotate and summarize. Again, if the teacher who is teaching the Scavenger Hunt needs assistance, the English teacher may be a natural choice. Annotating and summarizing are important concepts in most academic standards.

Learn to Search...Search to Learn

At the beginning, searching the Internet for relevant information can be one of life's more frustrating endeavors. Like all things, having a place to start is always helpful.

Common techniques that students should be familiar with are as follows:
- **plus (+)**: When placed before the keyword, it includes terms in your search topic.
- **minus (-)**: When placed before the keyword, it excludes terms (Inventors - automobiles).
- **Asterisk (*)**: When placed after a word, it acts like a wildcard (Invent*).
- **quotation marks ("")**: when quotation marks are placed around a phrase, the search will match results in that exact sequence ("characteristics of inventors").
- **(t:)** When placed before the keyword, it restricts the search to document titles (t: Thomas Edison).
- **u**: When placed before the keyword, it restricts the search to document URLs only (u: AltaVista).
- **Image**: It requests picture images having a specific filename. For example, use *image:thomas edison* to find pages with images called "Thomas Edison."

Although search engines do not accept all of these terms, these are standard protocols with which students and teachers should be familiar. Concentrate on one search engine as you learn what works best. Students may use a form to search and explore the various search engines, directories, or multi-search engines and to find out the special characteristics of each. A grid like the one on page 65 may be used to explore the various search engines and the benefits of each.

Inventors	Orville Wright-Wilbur	+t: Thomas Edison	Image: +Thomas +Edison
Yahoo! http://www.yahoo.com/			
Magellan http://www.mckinley.com/			
Hot Bot http://www.hotbot.com/			
Yahooligans! http://www.yahooligans.com/			
Searchopolis http://www.searchopolis.com			

In class, we then assign several activities that require teachers to really investigate a variety of search engines and to become familiar with the unique features of each. Teachers comment that having one search engine that they feel comfortable using makes creating activities, as well as directing students on how to use the Internet, a much easier process. The sample activity on page 67 helps teachers practice their search techniques.

Exploring Search Engines

1. What were the advanced features of each of the search engines you examined?

2. Did the search engines you examined provide filters to block unwanted Web sites? If so, how did the filters work for each search engine? Which ones were the most effective? Why?

3. What unique features did each search engine possess? Were these unique features useful? If so, why? If not, why not?

4. Was the search engine commercial in nature or was it student-oriented?

5. If you had to recommend one of the three search engines that you examined, which one would it be? Write your recommendation in two or three sentences.

6. Which search engine were you most comfortable using? Describe what made you feel more comfortable using that particular search engine than when you were using the others.

7. Be prepared to provide a two- or three-minute summary to the rest of the class about each of the search engines you examined.

Exhibit Center

This group of exhibits includes authentic examples of Scavenger Hunts. These activities are useful in teaching students how to use search engines both effectively and efficiently. To complete a Scavenger Hunt, students are required to raise their thinking to higher levels in Bloom's Taxonomy.

The following examples illustrate a wide variety of styles and difficulty levels. These Scavenger Hunts were developed with minimal knowledge of creating Web pages. These Scavenger Hunts have been completed so that the reader may more easily visualize the expected outcome.

Exhibit 5.1 | *Scavenger Hunt–Astronauts*

Scavenger Hunt—Astronauts

(This is a completed Scavenger Hunt.)

http://www.spa3.k12.sc.us/AstronautScavenger.htm
1. Describe the preparation an astronaut must undergo before making a flight into space.
2. Why was John Glenn's initial voyage into space such a significant event?
3. What is the significance of Glenn's most recent trip on the space shuttle?
4. What are some of the risks astronauts accept when traveling in space?

After you have completed your search, use the discovery form to present the material to the class.

Search Engine: **http://www.yahoo.com**

Keyword(s) or phrase(s) used to conduct search:
1. John Glenn
2. Astronauts
3. NASA Space Program
4. Kennedy Space Center
5. Preparing for Space Travel

Teacher's approval: _____
1. Address and brief description of site visited:
   URL: **http://spacelink.nasa.gov/NASA.Projects/Human. Exploration.and.Development.of.Space/Human.Space. Flight/Shuttle/Shuttle.Missions/Flight.092.STS-95/ John.Glenn.Returns.to.Space/**

Exhibit 5.1   *Scavenger Hunt–Astronauts* (*continued*)

Description: This site offers information on John Glenn's recent space shuttle mission. It discusses how the age barrier for astronauts has been broken as well as the tremendous physical demands that space travel places upon the human body.

2. Address and brief description of site visited:

   URL: **http://www.jsc.nasa.gov/bios/more.html**
   Description: This site provides a searchable biographical database of former and current U.S. astronauts and Soviet cosmonauts.

3. Address and brief description of site visited:
   URL: **http://www.nss.org/askastro/**

   Description: This site is an invaluable resource to directly contact current and former astronauts to have your questions answered. There is a database of former questions and answers that touch on hundreds of aspects of space travel, from preparation to space flight.

   What else did you find that you might wish to pursue at another time?
   One of the sites mentioned the new "educator astronauts," individuals from academic and teaching backgrounds who will eventually train for future missions. I would be interested in exploring the potential of these individuals to return to the classroom with invaluable, firsthand information about space travel.

Commentary: This example exhibits a completed Scavenger Hunt. The teacher begins the activity with a set of leading questions to help direct the students' inquiry. Following collaboration, a group of students generate a list of keywords and phrases that they had thought would be useful in searching for Web sites that contained information to answer the questions. The teacher extends the activity by requiring the students to present their finding in the form of an Internet Discovery *(see Chapter 7)*. After obtaining the teacher's signed approval, the students locate Web sites that they deem useful and record them in the space provided, accompanied by a brief summary. The learning objectives and assessment method are not provided in this activity but may have been explained in class prior to the Scavenger Hunt.

Exhibit 5.2   *Scavenger Hunt–Select a Decade*

Scavenger Hunt—Select a Decade

http://www.spa3.k12.sc.us/Scavdec.htm

<u>Objective:</u> Working in teams of four, conduct in-depth research on a particular decade.

<u>Task:</u> Select any resource approved by your teacher. Copy, paste, or rewrite to gather a pictorial history of your time period.
As a team, brainstorm ways in which to gather the information. The Internet may be used, but other materials and books may be used as well.
Students should cite the sources and Web sites that are used. Remember, you must ask permission to use other people's work. If they give you permission, you need to cite them as a source.

<u>Gather:</u> Select representative samples for each of the requested items.

<u>Evaluation:</u> Discuss the various artifacts from your decade. What appears to be the theme for the decade? What would be the differences between the decade you researched and the decade that you live in now? Which of the two decades do you think will make the most lasting difference to society? Why?

<u>Report:</u> Prepare a report presenting your findings during the evaluation to your classmate. *You may create a Web page, a multimedia presentation, a storyboard, or a scrapbook.*

<u>Grading:</u> How will you be graded on this assignment? Look at the scoring rubric at **http://www.spa3.k12.sc.us/Rubric.htm** before you begin the assignment.

<u>Gather the following:</u> Your group should document the URL. You may copy the artifact or provide a link for your team members.

Pictures of key political leaders

Artifacts from fads

A speech or a direct quote from a person who was alive during the decade

A sample of the clothing fashion of the time

An audio recording or the words of a hit song

A list of popular entertainment

Exhibit 5.2   *Scavenger Hunt–Select a Decade (continued)*

A list of popular sports

A painting from the decade

Three significant scientists or inventors of the time

The most significant advance during this time in science or in the humanities

Ten books published during this decade

Descriptions of the age by philosophers, writers, historians, politicians, and/or scientists

List three important businesses/industries during this period of time.

What ten items were made during this decade?

What war(s) or military conflicts were occurring?

Question: Discuss the various artifacts from your decade. What appears to be the theme for the decade? What would be the differences between the decade you researched and the decade that you live in now? Which of the two decades do you think will make the most lasting difference to society? Why?

Rubric

	Proficient	Competent	Basic
Understands Assignment	Distinguishes between relevant and irrelevant information; puts meaning of the problem in personal, social, or community perspective; understands the difference between decades/eras.	Includes relevant and irrelevant materials; uses limited number of sources; describes decade but does not reflect or relate information to decade in which he lives.	Links to sites and materials that are not directly connected to the assignment; uses one source; interprets meaning from one source; does not analyze or interpret artifacts that are collected.
Completes Assignment	Evaluates multiple artifacts; clearly and concisely draws conclusion from evidence; accesses and gathers appropriate material; gives appropriate citation to source; uses reliable sites.	Collected artifacts come from unidentified Internet sources; some artifacts are inappropriate and/or inaccurate; reliance on unreliable Internet sites.	Material collection is haphazard; student answers question(s) partially; does not attempt to make judgment or evaluation; artifacts are inappropriate or inaccurate.
Produces Product Connected to Assignment	Product clearly and coherently presents information; product is clearly related to task; information is accurate, organized, and polished. There is evidence of reflection, evaluation, and persistence.	Product produced is accurate, attractive, and organized. There is little reflection and evaluation of the materials by students; product is similar to other products that have been produced.	Product lists various artifacts; material is disorganized and unattractive; product is not clearly connected to the question.
Creativity	Student generates multiple approaches of looking at the problem; reflects on the uniqueness of each decade/era; demonstrates different approaches; product is unique and has clearly stretched the group's thinking.	Student demonstrates one clear approach to understanding the decade/era; compares decades/eras but does not draw conclusion.	Student copies and pastes from the Internet without discrimination; product demonstrates little connection to the question; product does not show reflection or evaluation.

Grade

Name of Student	Understands Assignment	Completes Assignment	Produces Product	Creativity	Overall Grade

Commentary: This Scavenger Hunt approaches the research from a broad perspective. Students are not limited to the Internet for acquiring resources and are given much leeway in gathering the required information. It is clear that there is a strong emphasis on collaboration in this activity; teams are required to brainstorm as well as to present reports to the class. The teacher *includes thought-provoking essential questions such as "Which of the two decades do you think will make the most lasting difference to society? Why?"* Students are informed up front that they will be graded based on a scoring rubric. Finally, students must provide documentation for the URLs they visit and provide links to the information they retrieve. Unlike more traditional formats, this Scavenger Hunt does not include a specific section where students provide the keywords they will be using for the search for the teacher's approval.

Exhibit 5.3	*Scavenger Hunt–Professional Athletes*

Scavenger Hunt—Professional Athletes

by Robin Breitenbach, Pam Cook, and Ann Hudson

http://www.spa3.k12.sc.us/WebQuests/Basketball/LangArts ScavHunt.html

- What training must an athlete have to become a professional?
- What are some risks associated with being a professional athlete?

Keeping these questions in mind, please focus on the language arts skills you will be using.

By completing this Scavenger Hunt, you will be able to:
- Examine broad ideas and narrow them down to specific topics
- Read for comprehension
- Summarize ideas and thoughts in your own words

Search Engine _____
Keyword(s) or phrase(s) used to conduct search:
1. _____
2. _____
3. _____
4. _____
5. _____

Don't forget to copy and paste your URLs (Web addresses) to a Word document and write a brief annotation for each site.

Exhibit 5.3   *Scavenger Hunt–Professional Athletes (continued)*

Evaluation: You will be evaluated based on the criteria listed in the following rubric.

Evaluation for Professional Athletes Scavenger Hunt

	Inadequate	Adequate	Good	Superior
Research	Much or most research information is inaccurate or incomplete.	Weak research information is used to support/ prove thesis.	Accurate and adequate research information is used to support thesis.	Accurate and thorough research information is used to support/ prove thesis
Content	Little, if any, development of supporting ideas is shown.	Ideas show a weak structure and do not flow smoothly.	All ideas are clearly written; some ideas may not support/ prove thesis appropriately.	All ideas are clearly written and flow logically to support/ prove thesis.
Conventions	Sentence structure, grammar, and punctuation show frequent and blatant errors; frequent misspelling of commonly used words.	Sentence structure, grammar, and punctuation demonstrate a basic understanding of mechanics; frequent minor errors in spelling.	Sentence structure, grammar, and punctuation demonstrate an adequate understanding of mechanics; infrequent, minor errors in spelling.	Sentence structure, grammar, and punctuation demonstrate proficiency of mechanics; minimal or no spelling errors.

Commentary: Here we see a Scavenger Hunt that focuses on language arts skills. Not only will students research the answers to leading questions about professional athletes, but they also will be practicing specific language arts skills, such as narrowing topics, reading for comprehension, and summarizing ideas. These teachers also provide some helpful directions to students who are engaged in this activity.

At the end of the activity, they remind the students to copy and paste (*see Chapter 4*) the URLs to a Microsoft Word document. This illustrates an important point. The Scavenger Hunt form may be a Web page created by a teacher and posted on the Internet, but students will need to transfer the information that they collect to another location, whether it be an electronic file or a piece of notebook paper. The teachers provide an evaluation rubric that explains the grading criteria. The point conversion for each mastery level would have been explained to the students prior to beginning the activity.

Exhibit 5.4 *Anne Frank Scavenger Hunt*

Anne Frank Scavenger Hunt

Adapted from a WebQuest by Jim Heffner, Polly Hembree, and Alicia Womick

http://www.spa3.k12.sc.us/scavengerhunts/frankscavengerhunt.htm

Essential Question: *Who was the most heroic historical figure of the 20th Century?*

Introduction: In studying our unit on World War II, we have examined the lives and actions of many exceptional leaders. Anne Frank, perhaps, was one of the most unlikely candidates to become a heroic figure. As you begin to gather research on the life of Anne Frank, consider the following questions:

- What was it like being a Jew in Europe from 1939-1945?
- How was someone like Adolph Hitler able to come into power?

Instructions: Using the search engine provided, identify at least three Web sites that you think will be useful in gathering information about World War II, specifically the Holocaust. When you have located a useful Web site, provide a brief written description of the site to explain why you think it is useful. To begin, on a separate sheet, work with your assigned group to generate five keywords that you will use to perform your Internet searches. Remember to obtain teacher approval before beginning your searches.

Search Engine _____

Keyword(s) or phrase(s) used to conduct search

1. _____
2. _____
3. _____
4. _____
5. _____

Teacher's approval: _____

1. Address and brief description of site visited: _____
2. Address and brief description of site visited: _____
3. Address and brief description of site visited: _____

Commentary: The Anne Frank Scavenger Hunt uses a broad essential question to focus the learning that will take place in this activity. Students would not be expected to answer the question "Who was the most heroic historical figure of the 20th Century?" in a Scavenger Hunt. This essential question was developed to be used throughout the Web-based learning framework and ultimately to be the basis for a WebQuest. The leading questions require the students to look at the life of Anne Frank in the wider context of the social and political culture of Europe during World War II.

Technical Corner

For technical assistance with the topics discussed in this chapter, please refer to the Appendix.

Skill	Description	Appendix Page Number
Chapter 5 Technical Corner		
What Is a Web Page?	Discusses importance of Web page as a means of sharing information and conveying clear content. Steps are outlined that demonstrate how to create Web pages from scratch or by using Web page templates.	188

Creating a Community of Learners: The Web Page

"Tell me and I'll forget. Show me and I'll remember. Involve me and I'll understand."
— *Confucius*

We have become a community of learners—sharing lesson plans, class assignments, and syllabi—across the Web. We have discovered that we have much in common. Using the Web, we are able to communicate with other educators on our own schedule through listservs, chatrooms, and e-mail.

Entire communities that support Web learning have sprouted. Blue Web'n **<http://www.kn.pacbell.com/wired/bluewebn/>** and Filamentality **<http://www.kn.pacbell.com/wired/fil/>** provide complete lesson showcases for those seeking assistance in developing Web-based learning projects.

The WebQuest page **<http://edWeb.sdsu.edu/Webquest/ Webquest.html)>** developed by Bernie Dodge, Tom March's Web and Flow **<http://www.ozline.com>**, and Kathy Schrock's Guide for Educators **<http://school.discovery.com/schrockguide/>** provide ready access to information that educators have developed and to the resources that we need to create our own outstanding lesson plans.

Students who were asked to suspend disbelief and view their teacher as the ultimate critic of all that was written are suddenly free to join the larger community of learners, and they are sharing their work and projects with others—other students, other teachers, other "real people." *"Why are we learning this?"* becomes *"How can I communicate this more clearly?"*

Research projects—created more often than not as part of a class exercise—are now posted on the Web and use learning tools to help other students know and understand a topic. No longer are the works of students—the traditional five- to 20-page research documentaries—hidden away in a student folder. The research may be a Web page or Web site that is posted on the Internet and shared with others who find the subject interesting.

Anyone who has access to the Web can become a publisher. Free Web-authoring tools and server space are available to allow anyone—even a person with minimal skills—to publish a document on the Web.

Process Step 3: Web Page

Just the thought of creating a **Web Page** was considered mystical only a few years ago. How did we ever get so many Web pages posted and allow people from across the world access to them? Surely the ability to do that must have taken some special power and know-how. How could an ordinary teacher become a part of this community of learners?

Web Page Conceptual Framework

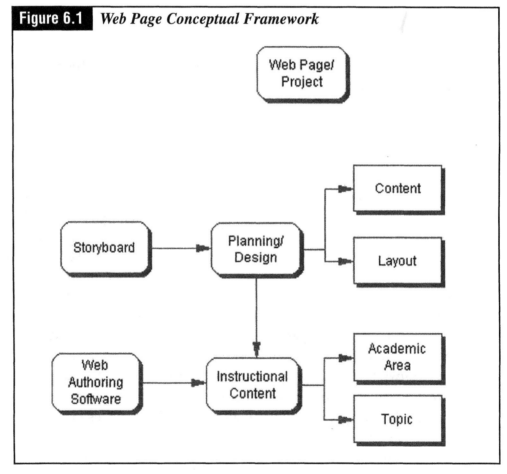

Figure 6.1 *Web Page Conceptual Framework*

This diagram was created using Inspiration® by Inspiration Software, Inc.

Web-authoring software is available for free. Of course, you can also write your own code. However, many teachers do not have the time or inclination to learn code when free software is available to write it. Netscape Navigator Gold and Microsoft FrontPage Express are both available free to educators. In addition, Microsoft Word and many of the new word processing programs convert documents to Web pages. For more complex effects, more sophisticated Web-authoring software can be purchased—such as FrontPage, DreamWeaver, or PageMaker. Remember, though, a Web page does not have to be sophisticated. Even the simplest page can be posted on the Web and viewed and enjoyed by millions of other Web users.

Basic Web page design and basic techniques for using Web-authoring tools should be introduced to the student before the project is underway. Bad design, such as excessive animation and misplaced pictures and text, will interfere with a project's usefulness for others. Remember that the primary purpose of creating a Web project or page is to communicate with others. Slow loading times and bad design impede communication as much as poor grammar and sentence structure impede written and oral communication.

As with all of the training we do, teachers and students begin the project by working with paper and pencil and deciding what they want and how they want to communicate an idea or topic. This is necessary preparation. If we don't have anything to say, communication stops. Before we create, we need to understand what we hope to accomplish. We need to ask ourselves, what is a Web page and what is the purpose?

What Is a Web Page or a Web Site?

When we use the term *the World Wide Web,* we are really referring to the millions and millions of Web pages that are posted for others to see. These pages are as different as the people who create them. Some contain graphics, audio or visual files, and animation. Other pages are clean and sparse. All are characterized by allowing us the opportunity to interact with information.

When there are related Web pages, we refer to them as a Web site. Each Web site has an index, an introductory page that is similar to a table of contents and leads the reader to move more deeply into the Web site. The teachers in the district in which we work usually keep their Web pages very simple. Most teachers will have several Web pages linked together. A typical teacher site may contain the following:

1. An index page that introduces the teacher and the class. Figure 6.2 is a typical example.

2. Links to subtopics.

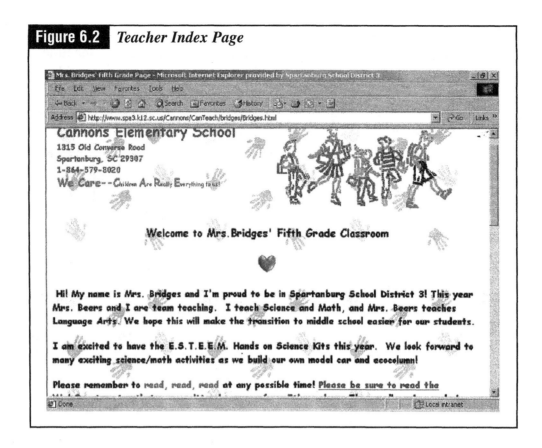

Figure 6.2 *Teacher Index Page*

Create a Storyboard

Before developing a Web site, a student or teacher needs to outline what will be communicated to visitors of the Web site. After all, that is the joy of the Web—communicating with others. A storyboard is a quick way for a group of students or teachers to determine the content of a Web site. One very quick way to brainstorm is to use sticky notes by attaching them to a whiteboard and drawing the connections or links between the individual pages. Sticky notes have another advantage—they can be easily moved and rearranged. The teacher Web site that we mentioned earlier could be outlined as shown in Figure 6.3.

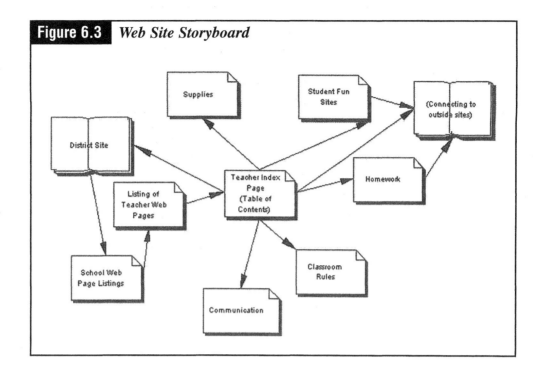

Figure 6.3 *Web Site Storyboard*

Or, the teacher could choose to hand out a paper like the storyboard sheet on page 82 and ask groups of students to work together and outline a Web site for the class or for a student project.

Web Page Storyboard

■ What is it that I want to say?

■ What arrangement of pages will I use to organize the Web site? (Web sites should have a hierarchical arrangement in which each element is categorized according to its importance.)

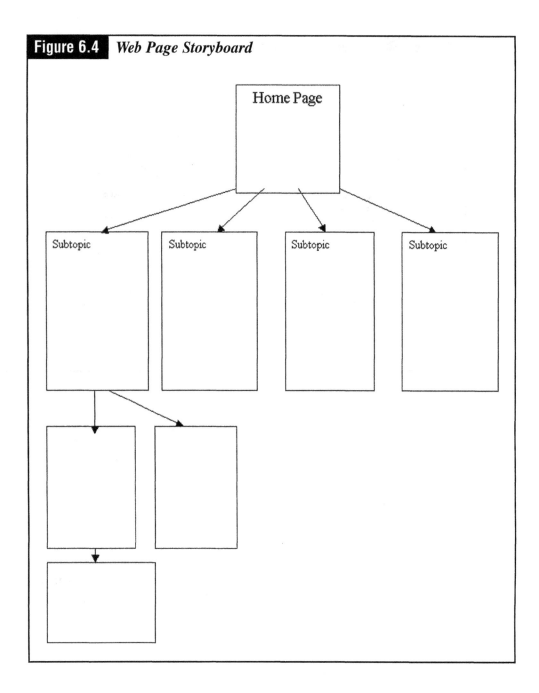

Figure 6.4 *Web Page Storyboard*

As the teacher works with students on a Web site, some design points may assist students as they make decisions. An important reminder is that Web visitors tend to "hit and run." If a visitor doesn't find something of immediate interest, the visitor does not stay to browse. Pages should not require extensive scrolling to read.

The Web is not designed for long reading tasks. Long pages require scrolling and that is only acceptable for information that will be read completely. For information that may be related but involves separate topics, the information should be broken into "chunks" that allow for easier access.

We also need to remember that Web visitors may wish to print the information—many people find it easier to read a hard copy of Web site information. The information should be broken down so that multiple topics are treated separately. This helps the viewer who may only want to print a single topic. How long is too long? While there is no specific rule for this, a good practice is to have primary information open immediately into the browser window. Also remember to limit the scrolling that a visitor must do—particularly on the entry page.

If we can separate the information, we will limit the amount of scrolling a visitor must do. In the interest of topic continuity, do not break up continuous information just to avoid scrolling. Think like a visitor to the site. Would a viewer want to read all of this information or just one topic? If the topic is broad with many subtopics, start a new page for each topic and provide an index page to let the viewer choose a hypertext link to surf to a topic with more information. A typical district site usually will include a link to schools instead of providing all of the information about each school in the district on the index page.

Guidelines for Designing a Web Site

As you work with students, there are several guiding principles that may assist them. As students work in groups, the task may be assigned in chunks. Roles may be defined as follows:

Public Information Specialist—One student may be required to decide on the image or theme the group will aim to project. Look at other schools and teachers' Web pages. What is well done? What needs improvement?

Designer—One student uses the storyboard to lay out the Web site. The designer also selects backgrounds, lines, colors, and pictures.

Writer—One student will determine what will be stated on the Web site. The text for each Web page must be written.

Working with a Learning Group

In facilitating a learning group that is creating a Web site, you may present guiding questions to focus the activity. The following assignments and questions may guide students in their work.

1. Complete a storyboard for a Web site for your district, school, classroom, or Web project. As you complete the storyboard, keep these questions in mind:
   (a) What information is the most important to communicate to the visitor? After determining the most important information, the students will know what information should be on the entry or index page.
   (b) What are some content chunks that you can separate? As the students work on separating a larger topic into subtopics, it will assist them to focus on what research they must do to communicate clearly.

(c) How can you avoid dull pages of solid text? Have you kept your paragraphs short? Are there some graphics to create interest?

(d) Are you directing the visitor's eye? When you look at the site, do design elements help your eye move easily from right to left, top to bottom?

2. Select one page from your storyboard that you think is particularly strong and design a Web page on paper.

3. Do you have a Guided Tour or a Scavenger Hunt that may be posted on the Web? Design a Web page for the Guided Tour. Share the Web page with your group; can it be made stronger? Clearer?

After a student or teacher has designed a Web page on paper, the next thing to do is to create an actual Web page, using the paper design as a guide.

Exhibit Center

Exhibit 6.1 | *What Is the Purpose of the Web Page?*

What Is the Purpose of the Web Page?

As you design your Web page, remind yourself of the purpose of the Web page. Ask yourself: *Why am I creating a Web page? What do I hope to communicate? With whom do I wish to communicate?*

Creating a Web Page—Decisions, Decisions
Before a student or teacher begins working on a Web site, there are several decisions that must be made. To review those decisions:

- Decide on the Web-authoring software that you will use to build your site. Popular software titles are Netscape Gold, Netscape Communicator, or FrontPage Express. (All are free to educators.) Claris Home Page, Microsoft Word, and Microsoft FrontPage are also available.
- Meet with parents and students as well as district, school, and community groups to assess what they envision for your school or district Web site. A group of people should carefully define site communication goals and organization, content categories, and responsibilities for content and site creation.
- Map out each page and determine how it will link.
- Assign areas of responsibility to specific individuals. Reach consensus on site design, usability, and content.
- One person should be in charge of content creation for each category (e.g., academic, testing, schools); another person should be in charge of site-wide creation and management.

Exhibit 6.1 *What Is the Purpose of the Web Page? (continued)*

Collect graphics, and design ideas. Explore other school sites.
- Web 66 provides links to school sites throughout the world. **http://Web66.coled.umn.edu/schools.html**

Royalty free clip art is available at many sites, including:
- About.com **http://Webclipart.miningco.com/**
- A+ Clip Art **http://aplusart.simplenet.com/aplusart/index.html**
- Microsoft Clipart Gallery **http://www.microsoft.com/clipgallery live/default.asp?ea=1**
- Barry's Clipart Service **http://www.barrysclipart.com/**

Design a basic theme for your site.
- Select a common logo. Most schools and districts have an identifying logo that is used for stationery or brochures and newsletters. If you prefer, you can add a banner or other identifying element to the top of your page.

Determine a basic color scheme or look. Web sites should project a similar resemblance—we are a family after all. FrontPage and other Web design products have standard themes that you may select or modify.
- Select identifying information to identify your site (e.g., name, address, telephone number).
- Insert a horizontal rule to separate the top of the site from the content.
- Limit the amount of scrolling that a person must do.
- Use tables where appropriate.
- Have a beginning, middle, and end.
- Use a friendly tone.
- Select basic navigation features for the bottom of the page.

Prepare content.
- Word, as well as other software, will automatically convert documents to HTML files. Use what you have. Typical information may include the course syllabus, homework assignments, class rules, projects, and samples of student work.
- Use pictures and other large files judiciously. Are they worth the wait?

Figure 6.5 | *Using a Common Logo for a Web Site*

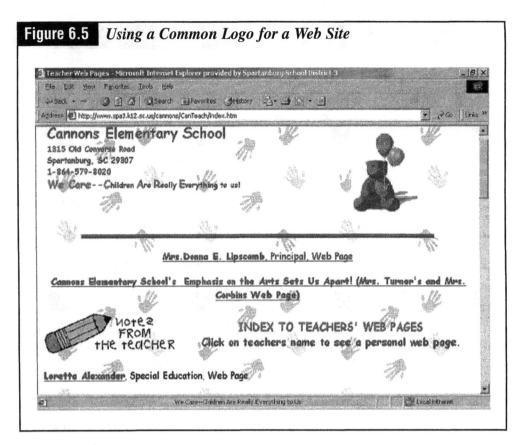

Microsoft® Internet Explorer 5.0 screen shot reprinted by permission from Microsoft Corporation.

Exhibit 6.2 | *Teacher Web Page Template*

Teacher Web Page Template

For teachers who have not grown up with the Internet, the whole notion of Web pages can seem foreign and intimidating. Rather than focus on all of the technical aspects of creating Web pages, we focus on the content and instructional purpose of a Web page.

We began to develop teacher Web page templates, which were pre-designed Web pages. We asked teachers to come to the workshop prepared with the content that they wished to include on their Web page. In this fashion, we were literally able to post the Web pages for an entire faculty within one day of the workshop.

Figure 6.6 is an example of one of the templates we have used. Teachers were asked to type in an introduction with pertinent information about themselves and the classes and subjects they teach. The template provides them with options to hyperlink to subordinate pages for things such as class rules, supplies, homework, and fun sites. If a teacher decides not to include content for multiple pages, we simply remove the links from the home page.

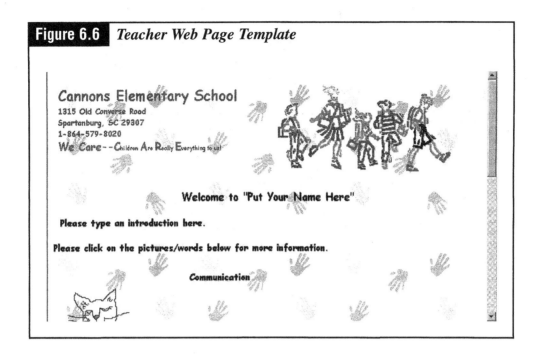

| Figure 6.6 | *Teacher Web Page Template* |

Commentary: Once teachers feel comfortable working with Web pages in general, they are often enthusiastic about using their Web page to facilitate instruction. Many teachers create hyperlinks from their personal Web page to a Guided Tour or Scavenger Hunt that they created in a workshop or class.

Technical Corner

For technical assistance with the topics discussed in this chapter, please refer to the Appendix.

Skill	Description	Appendix Page Number
Chapter 6 Technical Corner		
Creating Tables	Explains vital role tables play in creating Web pages and demonstrates how to create and modify tables.	191
Creating Links to Web Sites Using Text in MS Word 2000	Hyperlinks are the glue that connects Web pages to one another. This section demonstrates how to create hyperlinks to outside URLs.	192

Technical Corner (*continued*)

Skill	Description	Appendix Page Number
Chapter 6 Technical Corner		
Linking Pages in Your Web Project Using MS Word 2000	Linking together Web pages in a project is an important skill. Learn how to connect a multi-page Internet activity.	194
Posting Web Pages to a Web Site	Basic steps and resources are explained that will allow you and your students to publish your work on the World Wide Web.	195

Chapter 7

Exploring Information: An Internet Discovery

"All things must change to something new, to something strange."
— *Henry Wadsworth Longfellow*

Information has exploded. Every day we are bombarded with more information and images than we can process. Even more frightening is the fact that the information may be inaccurate. How do we teach students to sort, classify, and evaluate information? Not too many years ago, student access to information was limited by what was presented in class by teachers or in textbooks. Additionally, teachers, media specialists, and other professionals screened pre-selected materials—limiting purchased items to age-appropriate materials and those written by the most respected "experts."

Times have changed. Student access to information has exploded as a result of the World Wide Web and other electronic media. An Internet Discovery is one way to introduce students to finding, evaluating, and manipulating information. As with the traditional "research paper," an Internet Discovery allows a student to demonstrate his or her research ability and critical thinking skills. As education becomes more challenging and the information confronting us becomes more controversial, an Internet Discovery is a way to help students learn the skills necessary to produce reliable results.

Process Step 4: Internet Discovery

Although the Internet Discovery appears to be the easiest process step, it actually is more difficult than it appears because of the knowledge that a student must possess to make it a successful project. The Internet Discovery is designed for a student to construct his or her own learning.

Internet Discoveries are methods for directing independent student inquiry. Before the student is given the freedom for this Discovery, however, the teacher should feel confident that the individual is able to navigate *(see Chapter 4)*, search *(see Chapter 5)*, word process, create Web pages *(see Chapter 6)*, and use time wisely in the quest for information.

Additionally, the teacher must ascertain that the student is able to evaluate Web sites for accuracy. Students need to look at information found on the Web with a healthy skepticism. Many students have a heartfelt belief that if something is written or widely disseminated than it has to be correct. For a teacher, helping students overcome these misconceptions is a daunting task.

Many adults are unable to assess the accuracy and usefulness of a Web site. For that matter, assessing the accuracy and usefulness of any media—be it television, newspaper, or magazine—is a skill many Americans lack, no matter what their age. Why should the World Wide Web be any different?

Internet Discovery Conceptual Framework

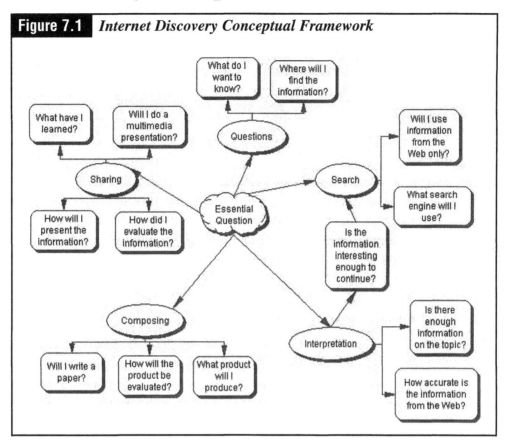

Figure 7.1 *Internet Discovery Conceptual Framework*

This diagram was created using Inspiration® by Inspiration Software, Inc.

Structure of the Internet Discovery

An Internet Discovery consists of five basic phases that are reviewed by the teacher before the student proceeds with the research. These phases are *question, search, interpretation, composition,* and *sharing.*

> *Question*—What is it that the student wishes to research?
> *Search*—How will the topic be researched?
> *Interpretation*—What documenting information will the student look for as the topic is researched?
> *Composition*—What will be written? How will it be presented?
> *Sharing*—How will the student share the information with other students?

Five Phases of Discovery

The first phase is the **question**. A student decides, with the assistance of the teacher, what he or she would like to explore further, related to the current unit of study. Before the student meets with the teacher, the student will have conducted preliminary research. The purpose of the research is to provide the student an opportunity to learn enough about the topic to frame several questions that might prove interesting.

During the meeting with the teacher, the student shares the questions, and the student and teacher speculate as to what direction the research may go. The teacher approves all questions in advance of the search.

The second phase is the **search**. The search may involve looking for information on the Internet or in the media center, or it may involve searching for demonstrations and experiments to illustrate a unit of study. The teacher suggests other ways to search for information. The Web site evaluation form is used as a discussion point for emphasizing the importance of the student verifying information. Together, the student and the teacher determine how the student will document the research. For example, *"Will the student take notes from these resources and prepare a traditional bibliography, or will the student print out important resources?"* An older student may be required to maintain a complete bibliographic file while a younger student may print out portions of a Web site that provide background information.

The third phase is **interpretation**. After the meeting with the teacher, the student continues the preliminary research begun during the initial question phase. The student sifts through additional information that has been gathered, and refines the questions through documenting information.

The fourth phase is **composition**. This may involve a combination of products that the student agrees to present. Is the information such that a written summary of the information would be the most effective means to deliver the information? Would a PowerPoint or HyperStudio presentation be the best means to deliver the information? Would the student prefer to deliver an oral report or a poster board display?

How Will the Work Be Evaluated?

It is during the composition phase that the student and the teacher reach agreement as to how the work will be evaluated. Will a rubric be used? Will peer evaluation be used?

In the sample rubric on page 93, the teacher emphasizes the necessity for the student to use the information in a reflective and analytical fashion. For example, if the student uses a limited number of sites, the level of competence is Basic. If the student uses multiple sites and manipulates the information, however, the level rises to Competent. Furthermore, if the product that the student produces is clearly related to the topic and if the student has analyzed and evaluated the information, the competency level is Proficient.

Sample Rubric

	Proficient	Competent	Basic
Understands Assignment	Distinguishes between relevant and irrelevant information; uses the information in a new way; relates the information to what is studied; analyzes or interprets information in an interesting manner.	Includes relevant and irrelevant materials; uses limited number of sources; does not reflect or relate information to subject being studied.	Links to sites and materials that are not directly connected to the assignment; uses one source; interprets meaning from one source.
Completes Assignment	Evaluates multiple artifacts; clearly and concisely draws conclusion from evidence; accesses and gathers appropriate material; gives appropriate citation to source; uses reliable sites.	Collected information comes from unidentified Internet sources; some information is inappropriate and/or inaccurate; begins to make judgment or evaluation.	Material collection is haphazard; student answers question(s) partially.
Produces Product Connected to Assignment	Product clearly and coherently presents information; product is clearly related to task; information is accurate, organized, and polished; there is evidence of reflection, evaluation, and persistence.	Product produced is accurate, attractive, and organized. There is little reflection and evaluation of the materials by students; product is similar to other products that have been produced.	Material is disorganized and unattractive; product is not clearly connected to the question; product is a rehash of one source.
Creativity	Student generates multiple approaches of looking at the problem; product is unique and has clearly stretched the student's thinking.	Student demonstrates one clear approach to understanding the information; compares information but does not draw conclusion.	Student copies and pastes from the Internet without discrimination; product demonstrates little connection to the question.

The fifth phase of the Internet Discovery is **sharing**. This is a way for students to collaborate and to share search and navigation techniques that they have learned. As students discuss what they have learned and how they have learned it, it becomes a review of good Web techniques. With the teacher stressing multiple sites and multiple resources, inevitably there will be a conflict in the information presented. How did the student determine which set of information to believe? Through the collaboration, each student becomes an expert.

The teacher may construct a form to provide students a basis for determining whether or not a Web site is reputable and is likely to have accurate information. Some of the questions that we must encourage students to ask are:

"Who is the author?"
"Who is the intended audience?"
"What is the author's experience with the topic?"
"Why was the information gathered?
"Is the information up-to-date?"
"Does the author have a motive for posting the information?"
"Are there credible links to other sites?"

The form need not be elaborate or complex. A clear, easy-to-use guide should provide students with enough structure to make sound decisions about the material that they will be evaluating.

Web Site Review

Topic researched _____
_____

Name of Web site/URL _____
_____

Sponsoring organization/individual_____
_____

Who is the authority for the site? _____

Can you e-mail someone at the site? _____

Does the site link with other sites? If so, what is the content of those sites?
_____
_____

Are the sites that are linked to the original site related to the topic and accurate?
_____
_____

Does it credit any source for the information? If so, who is credited? Is the credited
source generally reliable? _____
_____
_____
_____
_____
_____

What graphics are there on the site? Are they well done? _____
_____

Is the site easy to use? _____

After students become experienced with using the Web through Guided Tours and Scavenger Hunts, they may be ready to research information on the Web. Although it's not a traditional research paper, the Internet Discovery is product-oriented. The student must answer the questions "What am I looking for?" and "How will I present it to others?" The Internet Discovery may be part of a Jigsaw *(see Chapter 2)* where a student collects additional information, manipulates the information, and shares it with classmates.

The Internet Discovery provides an ideal venue for students to dig more deeply into a subject that has been introduced by the teacher through discussion, a Guided Tour, or a Scavenger Hunt. Frequently, it is an outcropping of a student's natural curiosity—the student may find a site on the Web or information on the Web that captures the imagination.

The purpose of the Discovery Form is to focus the student's research efforts. As with any project, a teacher controls the research to ensure student success. Just as a teacher reviews the basic Web research paper techniques beforehand—narrowing of topic, note cards, outlining, and bibliography—the teacher reviews basic research techniques with the student. Before the Internet Discovery is approved, the teacher and the student go over the fundamentals:

- Is the topic sufficiently narrowed to produce valuable results?
- Does the student have a grasp of what belongs with the topic and what veers away from the topic?
- Does the student have a clear idea of where to search for information?
- Does the student have a clear idea as to how the information will be presented to the class?
- How will the project be evaluated?

Internet Discovery Form

The purpose of this form is to assist you in brainstorming an idea to research. Before any research begins, you must decide what you wish to explore. You will also need to think about the keywords that you will use to search the Web. Be sure you get the teacher's approval before proceeding with the next step in the project.

Name _____ Date_____

Title of the Internet Discovery _____

The purpose of the project is to _____

_____

Questions that I would like to answer in the discovery:
1. _____
2. _____
3. _____
4. _____

Search engine or directory that I will use _____

Keyword(s) or phrase(s) that I will use to conduct the search:
1. _____
2. _____
3. _____
4. _____
5. _____

Teacher approval (Teacher must initial before searching may begin.) _____

Interesting questions that should be added to the discovery:
1. _____
2. _____
3. _____

I will do the following with this project information:
1. _____
2. _____

I will be evaluated by:
1. _____
2. _____

Teacher approval (Teacher must initial before student begins composing.) _____

I plan to use the following additional resources:
1. _____
2. _____
3. _____
4. _____
5. _____

I will present the information in the following manner:
1. _____
2. _____

Since the topic and the research materials are pre-approved, there is little chance for surprise in the end result. Notice, the teacher agrees up front with suggested ways that the student will use and present the information.

By providing students with a wider range of options for uncovering information and displaying their knowledge, we accommodate the many different ways our students learn. Through classroom discussion, one-on-one conferencing, and pre-research, the student should be able to define the purpose of a topic that will be interesting and informative. The student may decide to look at the topic from a different viewpoint than the teacher envisioned.

However, if the teacher has prepared the groundwork through the Scavenger Hunt *(see Chapter 5)*, the students will have these skills before ever reaching this step. Students should receive a great deal of practice in defining search terms before the Internet Discovery is attempted. They should also be able to evaluate Web sites. By ensuring that some Web site evaluation procedure has been presented to the student, the teacher will avoid this problem.

Encountering sites that are misleading, inaccurate, or prejudicial will likely occur as students search for information. It is vital, however, that students are taught how to react when they venture to sites that are inappropriate, deceptive, or malicious. There is no better place than school for a student to learn the information-gathering skills necessary in today's society.

Finally, an Internet Discovery calls for the student to explain how the information will be presented. Again, this is a point of departure. Generally, we ask that projects be presented in the same manner. While that is an excellent technique when we are teaching students how to create a certain model, if the emphasis is on information collected rather than the form of the product, multiple presentation forms are appropriate.

Student projects take the form appropriate to the information collected. The information may best be presented as a Web page or site, PowerPoint presentation, WebQuest, Guided Tour, CyberInquiry, or traditional research paper. Since the student and teacher determine in advance how the information will be evaluated, there will be an expectation of what the final product should be and how the student is expected to use the collected information.

Once the Internet Discovery Form is completed by the student, it becomes an opportunity for a student and teacher to meet and discuss what the learning objectives are and how the student intends to meet those objectives. It is through these discussions that a suitable topic is developed. Because of the limited knowledge that a student brings to a research topic, a teacher needs to guide and refine the student's search for information to ensure success.

Exhibit Center

Internet Discoveries serve as learning transitions for students to develop an in-depth understanding on a given topic. The examples in this section include completed Internet Discovery Forms that illustrate a wide variety of directions that these activities can take.

Internet Discoveries are rich with potential for teaching students how to evaluate material and how to use information effectively. The richness derives from the conversation that a student and a teacher have regarding basic research techniques. Students need the focus and direction of a teacher, particularly during the introductory phases of research. However, the student must first conduct the preliminary research and think about how he or she could use information.

Following each exhibit in this section, we have provided a commentary on areas of discussion that would occur between the student and the teacher. The completion of the form is not the purpose of the Internet Discovery. The form is a springboard that allows a student and a teacher to conduct a dialogue about the best way to present information.

Exhibit 7.1 *Astronaut Discovery Form*

Astronaut Discovery Form

In 1998, Senator John Glenn became the oldest man to travel in space. This topic made for good discussion in schools. It was very easy for teachers and students to tie some aspect of the space flight into the curriculum. An Internet Discovery on John Glenn's historic trip into space may appear as follows:

Name: <u>Suzy Smith</u>
Date: <u>November 8, 1998</u>
Title of the Internet Discovery: **The Aging Effects of Space Travel on the Human Body; Making Space Travel Safe for the Elderly**
Keyword(s) or phrase(s) used to conduct search:
1. John Glenn
2. Astronauts
3. NASA Space Program
4. Kennedy Space Center
5. Preparing for Space Travel

<u>Interesting topics that I discovered and would like to explore further:</u>
I found the connection between John Glenn's breaking the age barrier in space travel and greater opportunities in space flight now afforded women as a direct result worthy of additional exploration.

Exhibit 7.1 *Astronaut Discovery Form (continued)*

<u>What is the purpose of the project?</u> The purpose of this project is to iden-tify the debilitating effects of space travel on healthy human specimens. More specifically, the project will examine how space travel mimics the effects of aging on bones, circulation, and other human biological sys-tems.

<u>What do I find interesting that I would like to present to my classmates?</u> I would like to present the possibilities of how we can improve space travel safety for all individuals, with a special focus on the elderly.

Teacher Approval: _____

Interesting questions that should be added to the Discovery:
  1. Why does zero gravity promote bone loss in all individuals trav-eling in space?
  2. What is the longest estimated length of time an elderly (over age 70) individual could spend in space without incurring irre-versible biological damage?
  3. Do the medical benefits of studying the effects of space travel on the elderly outweigh the risks imposed on such individuals?

I plan to use the following additional resources:
  1. *Grolier's CD Encyclopedia*
  2. The school and public library
  3. Multimedia clips of John Glenn answering questions while in space
  4. Scale models of the space shuttle and previous rockets

I will present the information in the following manner:
  1. I will create a PowerPoint presentation and provide handouts for the entire class.
  2. I will use models of spaceships to emulate the orbit trajectory around the Earth.

Commentary: The student has done a very nice job of doing preliminary research on the effects of space travel. While some of the questions in the Internet Discovery are focused on the knowledge level, Question 3 (Do the medical benefits of studying the effects of space travel on the elderly out-weigh the risks imposed on such individuals?) provides a rich area to research. The teacher would very likely redirect the student to emphasize that part of the Internet Discovery.

The products that the student proposes to produce are only peripherally related. Since the purpose of this Internet Discovery is to focus on the medical benefits of space travel on the elderly, the student should probably discard the idea of using models of spaceships to emulate the orbit trajectory around the Earth. That is not directly related to the topic being researched.

The student and teacher may determine that it would be best to list the PowerPoint presentation and the handout separately. That would be particularly true if both were being evaluated. Is the handout merely an extension of the PowerPoint show or will it provide supplemental material? That should be determined before the student continues the research.

Exhibit 7.2 *Decade of Discovery—The 1960s*

Decade of Discovery—The 1960s

When studying a unit as rich and diverse as the 1960s, an Internet Discovery is an excellent vehicle for enabling students to probe deeper into issues and events that might not receive significant time in class.

Title of the Internet Discovery: "You Say You Want a Revolution?"

Keyword(s) or phrase(s) used to conduct search:
1. Martin Luther King, Jr.
2. John F. Kennedy
3. The Vietnam War
4. Anti-War Protests
5. The Beatles

<u>Interesting topics that I discovered and would like to explore further:</u>
When we completed the Scavenger Hunt on the 1960s, I became really interested in learning more about the involvement of the United States in the Vietnam War. I also found information about anti-war protests in the music of the era that I would like to explore.

<u>What is the purpose of the project?</u> The purpose of this project is to discover why the United States fought in Vietnam for so many years even though there was a great deal of opposition to the war by American citizens.

<u>What do I find interesting that I would like to present to my classmates?</u>
I would like to present a couple of anti-war songs that were popular in the 1960s. One, "Revolution," by the Beatles didn't specifically mention the Vietnam War but kind of reflected the general attitude of the younger generation growing up in the 1960s. Also, I want to look at Bob Dylan's song, "The Times They are A-Changin."

Exhibit 7.2 | *Decade of Discovery—The 1960s* (continued)

Teacher Approval: _____

Interesting questions that should be added to the discovery:
1. What effect did popular music have on the anti-war movement?
2. How did music play a role in the lives of American soldiers stationed in Vietnam?

I plan to use the following additional resources:
1. The school's CD-ROM library
2. Online music resources

I will present the information in the following manner:
1. I am going to use PowerPoint to copy and paste the lyrics of anti-war songs and add graphics to the slides.
2. I plan to explain the meaning of these songs as well as their significance to the anti-war movement.

Commentary: A teacher reviewing this Internet Discovery proposal would make suggestions to focus the learning. The search terms indicate an interest in the 1960s; however, the proposal does not indicate a narrowing of the subject to the Vietnam War. The student indicates that the research would focus on the Vietnam War and on anti-war music in the 1960s. The latter topic would probably be a more "doable" topic.

In order to focus on that topic, the student would then have to predetermine the purpose of the project. Why the United States fought the Vietnam War is not particularly relevant to anti-war protest songs. Furthermore, the student's idea to present lyrics from songs dealing with the anti-war protest movement is acceptable, but it lacks depth. By reviewing a rubric, the teacher may direct the student to use the information more effectively.

Additionally, the student shows interest in examining the role of the United States in the Vietnam War. Looking at a couple of song lyrics would not accomplish this learning objective. Together, the teacher and student would explore other ways that the objective could be accomplished.

As an alternative, it may be necessary for this student to expand the scope of the Internet Discovery to research other pertinent information. A student may begin to speculate about broad topics such as the political climate of America during the 1960s, global political changes, and the spread of communism. The teacher also could suggest that a student explore the vital and strategic interests that compelled the United States to become embroiled in the decade-long conflict.

Decisions on what to research in an Internet Discovery are determined by the topic and the academic standards that are being taught. The teacher's role is to direct the student around all of the distracting information sources that are on the Web. This Internet Discovery on the 1960s is fairly typical of student work during the early phases of research. The conference between the teacher and the student will help the student move around the barriers.

Exhibit 7.3 *Discovery Form–Anne Frank*

Discovery Form—Anne Frank

When dealing with an emotional instructional unit like the Holocaust, Internet Discoveries can provide an opportunity for students to reflect. For a topic that is as overwhelming as the Holocaust, students need time to ask questions to clarify how a civilized nation could let something like that occur.

Title of the Internet Discovery: **The Historical Importance of Anne Frank's Diary**

Keyword(s) or phrase(s) used to conduct search:
1. Diary +"Anne Frank"
2. Holocaust
3. "World War II" + Holocaust
4. Jews + Holocaust
5. Anne Frank

Interesting topics that I discovered and would like to explore further:
I would like to find out more about the families and individuals who hid Jews and other groups persecuted by Nazi Germany.

What is the purpose of the project?
I want to show how Anne Frank and her family were able to hide in an attic for years while avoiding being found by Nazi troops. I would also like to explain to the class how people could become swept up in a movement even if they personally know that it is wrong.

What do I find interesting that I would like to present to my classmates?
There have been certain groups that claim that the diary was a hoax and was not authentic. I would like to present evidence that proves that the diary is an accurate account of the events described by Anne Frank.

Teacher Approval: _____

Exhibit 7.3 *Discovery Form–Anne Frank (continued)*

Interesting questions that should be added to the discovery:
1. Who betrayed the Franks' hiding place to the Nazis?
2. What factors made normal people assist the Nazis in carrying out their persecution and murder of millions of innocent people?

I plan to use the following additional resources:
1. Annotated list of Web sites from Scavenger Hunt
2. The school library
3. Scanned pages of Anne Frank's Diary
4. Magazine articles about Anne Frank

I will present the information in the following manner:
1. I plan to use Microsoft Publisher and Microsoft Word to create a diary. I will interview Holocaust survivors through e-mail and use their stories in the diary.

Commentary: This Internet Discovery proposal clearly displays more clarity and purpose than the two previous examples. It is unlikely that the student was able to develop and articulate these ideas on the first try. The questions that are raised in this proposal hint at considerable reflection on the student's part as well as a strong prior understanding of the events and circumstances influencing the life of Anne Frank.

The New Research: A CyberInquiry

"I cannot teach anybody anything; I can only make them think."
— *Socrates*

A CyberInquiry and a WebQuest *(see Chapter 9)* are research models that focus on how students use information. While the models may ask that students look for additional information, the emphasis is placed upon "the student as researcher" and on how a student looks at information critically. Building upon the Guided Tour, the Scavenger Hunt, and the Internet Discovery models, the Inquiry and the WebQuest provide lists of collected Web sites for students to explore. The collected Web sites serve both as a springboard for students to pursue additional work on the topic and for students to manipulate the information and problem solve.

At face value, the CyberInquiry contains many more components than the previous four process steps. Fortunately, the technical skills required for the CyberInquiry are not any more difficult than for a Web page or Guided Tour. However, With the focus on problem solving, however, the content of a CyberInquiry is more rigorous than the earlier process steps.

It is helpful to understand the differences between a CyberInquiry and a WebQuest and the distinct challenges of each. The most prominent difference between the two activities is that a CyberInquiry is more linear than a WebQuest. The CyberInquiry—much like the WebQuest—broadens the curriculum from textbook-centered material to real-world applications, including simulations, demonstrations, and community learning. While WebQuests contain roles that are frequently at odds with one another, a CyberInquiry does not. After our first year of modeling WebQuests for teachers, we saw that although many of the activities were valuable instructionally, they were not WebQuests.

The CyberInquiry focuses on individual exploration and writing. Individuals in cooperative learning groups study a broad topic, such as the Holocaust or the 1960s *(see the Exhibit Center at the end of this chapter)*. The intellectual struggle with an essential question—such as "Who are the Heroes?"—encourages interaction with information. Each student within the learning group contributes to an ever-growing portfolio of information pertaining to the question.

One of the most advantageous characteristics of a CyberInquiry is that it can progress into a fully developed WebQuest. Once a teacher tests a CyberInquiry with a class during one semester, it is possible to take the materials gathered in the portfolio and expand them to include varying viewpoints. Furthermore, students will likely possess a more complete knowledge base to pull from when engaged in the WebQuest.

Process Step 5: CyberInquiry

A CyberInquiry is a transition step between a Guided Tour and a WebQuest. Like the WebQuest, the CyberInquiry requires that students analyze, synthesize, and evaluate. The student is challenged to think critically in order to solve a task. Although it is a transition, it has a depth and credibility of its own as a learning activity.

The CyberInquiry has an overview, an introduction, an investigation, gathering and sorting, and an evaluation. The CyberInquiry is linear—students struggle with an essential question and respond to it. The teacher provides background material for the investigation, and students generate additional research. In a CyberInquiry, students manipulate information. Frequently, a student uses the structure of a CyberInquiry to present information found in an Internet Discovery to classmates. Or a teacher may develop the CyberInquiry from the hotlists, Guided Tours, and Scavenger Hunts created previously from introductory learning on a topic.

CyberInquiry Conceptual Framework

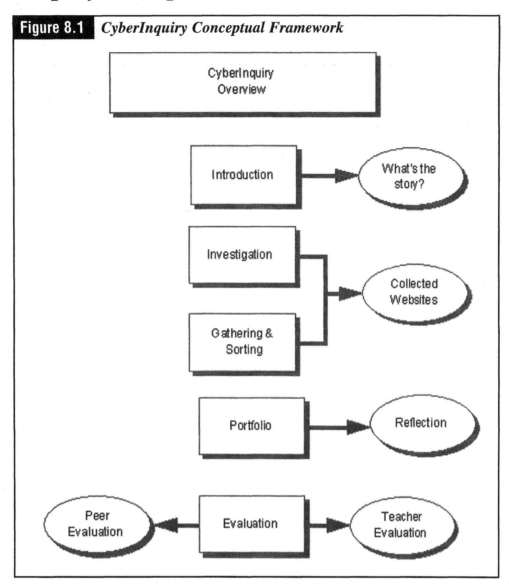

Figure 8.1 *CyberInquiry Conceptual Framework*

This diagram was created using Inspiration® by Inspiration Software, Inc.

Creating a CyberInquiry

There are five basic steps to creating a CyberInquiry: **introduction, investigation, gathering and sorting, creating a portfolio**, and **evaluation**.

Before beginning a CyberInquiry, the teacher always creates the overview or teacher notes. First, the overview centers the lesson clearly on the grade-level academic standards that the Inquiry will address. Second, the overview provides a quick summary of what the Inquiry is to accomplish instructionally.

The first step is the **introduction**. The introduction captures the student's attention with simulation or a real-world quandary to solve. It contains an essential question *(as discussed in Chapter 3)*. The essential question allows us to spiral learning. A question that spirals learning builds from the student's previous learning, connects to an application of that learning, and extends to new information. The essential question shapes our response to information, prodding students to evaluate and establish a context for the content.

Major issues, problems, concerns, interests, or themes are fertile content for essential questions. The CyberInquiry introduction may be:

"As part of a Public Broadcasting series on the new millennium, you have been asked to produce an overview of the 1960s that explores the questions, 'Why were the 1960s so contradictory?' and 'Why were peace and love such common themes?' Your production is limited to 15 minutes."

Or the introduction may focus on the essential question itself: *"Who were the heroes in the Holocaust? Were the children of the Holocaust heroic, or were they dealing with their circumstances in the best way that they could?"*

The second step is the **investigation**. The investigation provides the background links for students to explore. This provides common background for all students. The hotlists (lists of Web sites that are annotated) usually have been collected over a period of time and very often have been used to create a Guided Tour. In the investigation, the teacher structures background information—including collected Web sites—that students must know and understand in order to begin working on the task. If appropriate, the teacher will also provide historical or cultural perspective.

As part of the investigation, a writing activity will likely be required. A writing activity provides a framework for response to the essential question. It is a valuable individual product for students since it encourages a student to process and manipulate the information collected.

After the completion of the writing activity or other processing activity, students present their findings to their cooperative learning group. They may use charts, flowcharts, or other means to present this information. After students in the group have presented their findings, the group reaches a consensus about the information that should be presented to the entire class. The group determines the direction for further research or begins to organize the information for presentation.

The third step entails **gathering and sorting**. Students collect additional information that will assist them as they explore the scenario more fully. Since the group members may decide that they wish to dig more deeply into an area in which the collected Web sites are insufficient, additional Web searching may take place.

The fourth step is the **portfolio**. The teacher or the student who has created a CyberInquiry also creates the portfolio—a colorfully decorated crate or multi-pocketed file with supplemental information (e.g., magazine articles, artifacts, bibliographies of library materials). The student researches the materials for additional information to add to his or her upcoming presentation.

In addition, each student reviews the material that has been collected through the background Web sites and determines what is "the best" or the "most interesting" information. The material cannot duplicate information that is already placed in the portfolio.

The student may leave a predetermined number of items in the portfolio. (It's important that students make a judgment.) Once the selections are made, the student annotates an index card and attaches it to each selection, providing an explanation about why that information was selected to enrich the portfolio. The portfolio stays in the classroom and continues to grow as students complete the CyberInquiry. As a consequence, selection of material to add to the portfolio requires more and more reflection as the portfolio grows.

The fifth step is **evaluation**. The cooperative learning group reconvenes and shares the additional information that each person has collected. This Jigsaw is important to the group's work. Each group produces a product, which may be a multimedia presentation or the development of a Web site. Produced according to the pre-established rubric criteria, the product is evaluated by the teacher.

Eventually, the group uses the product as part of a presentation to the entire class. The presentation must provide enough background information so that all classmates gain an understanding of the topic. The presentation is evaluated by classmates, according to a peer evaluation rubric developed by the teacher or by the group itself.

Using the CyberInquiry Template

The CyberInquiry Template is useful for "walking" the first-time user through the steps of a CyberInquiry. In using the template, we ask that the multidisciplinary team of teachers—two- to four-member teams work well—highlight the text instructions and replace them with the appropriate information. For example, the first text instruction asks the team to "describe what the lesson is about." We ask that the teacher highlight that text and replace it with the description.

The template is a method for step-by-step instruction. It provides a reminder of the key components that are needed for a CyberInquiry. The template also encourages a teacher to include key components that will lead to a WebQuest. The Jigsaw, for example, provides an opportunity for the teacher to become comfortable having students research several different aspects of a topic and then reunite and share that information with other students.

Sample Template

Put the Title of the CyberInquiry Here

Developed by (put your name, an e-mail link, and your URL)

Overview

Describe what the lesson is about.

Specify content area (e.g., mathematics, language arts) and grade level (e.g., middle, elementary, early childhood).

Specify strands and objectives from the grade-level curriculum standards that will be addressed by the CyberInquiry. List by subject area.

List any special resources that a teacher would need in the classroom or in the media center for the students to complete the activity—for example, print resources in the media center, art reproductions, or video and audio materials.

Introduction

Write an introduction that gives students background about the topic. Try to interest them. What is a real-world topic that may interest them?

- What are the essential questions that students should analyze? (Note: The question(s) should encourage student interpretation and should allow for various answers.)

Example: If studying a unit on John Glenn's recent journey into space, an essential question could be, *"Despite the potential advances in medicine, should the elderly be allowed/encouraged to participate in space flights, which may be potentially harmful to the human biological systems, especially in the elderly?"*

Or, if studying a unit on earthquakes, the essential question could be, *"What would people need to do to increase their chances of surviving an earthquake?"*

Investigation

The investigation should orient students to the material that they will be studying. The CyberInquiry developer provides the researched Web sites (URLs) that will provide common background material necessary to explore the essential question(s). Brief, concise annotations will be added to let students know what information the Web site contains.

1. Collected Web sites

Following are Web sites students may explore about space travel:

http://www.nasa.gov
Description: Visit NASA's home page to gather information about the effects of space travel on the human body.

http://spacelink.nasa.gov/NASA.Projects/Human.Exploration.and.Development.of.Space/ Human.Space.Flight/Shuttle/Shuttle.Missions/Flight.092.STS-95/John.Glenn.Returns.to.Space/
Description: This site offers information on John Glenn's recent space shuttle mission. It discusses how the age barrier for astronauts has been broken as well as the tremendous physical demands that space travel places upon the human body.

Provide an activity sheet that questions students about information from the Web sites and identifies areas they may need to be reviewed.

2. Information on Historical/Cultural Perspective

- Provide guiding question(s) that look at main question(s) from a historical/cultural perspective. For instance, *"How has the perception of the elderly changed over the past century?"*

- Instruct students to rephrase the essential question(s) and to suggest an Internet Inquiry they might be interested in developing that compares the historical or cultural time.

3. Writing Activity

Writing activities are outstanding for encouraging students to organize and to use information in a new way. As students research the collected sites, they should be taking sufficient notes to react to the information. Instruct students before they begin researching sites that they will be required to write an argumentative essay/paper addressing the essential question(s).

Provide a rubric to assist students as they write their papers.

Each group member generates his or her own essay.

4. Jigsaw

Students return to their cooperative learning groups and prepare a presentation for the group on the information that they have collected that is relevant to the essential question that the group is discussing.

Students present their information to the group by:
- Charts
- Flowcharts
- Graphic organizer
- PowerPoint presentation
- Essay or other means to present this information

Consensus: The group determines the direction for further research or organizes the information for presentation to the entire class.

Gathering & Sorting

Gathering:
Students list and annotate Web sites that further explain the essential question(s).

Sorting:
Students sort through the information that they have collected and organize it into categories. Information that will be helpful in the group presentation is separated and made ready.

Identification of other resources that may be used to complete the task(s). Other resources may include:
- PowerPoint software to develop an informative slideshow
- Any URL links provided in this section
- Classroom encyclopedias
- Color printer
- Periodicals from the Media Center

Portfolio

As part of a CyberInquiry, a brightly decorated portfolio—perhaps a crate or a box—is created that contains supplementary information.

The portfolio could be a brightly decorated box or bin and may contain materials such as library books, biographies, articles, magazines, models, artifacts, bibliographies, and other materials that may be useful in studying the topic further.

Students should be given ample opportunity to explore the materials contained in the portfolio. Materials should be added to the portfolio.

Select the "most interesting" or the "best" of the materials created (no more than two selections). Do not duplicate anything in the box.

Add selection(s) to the box. Attach an index card to the material and explain the reason for the selection.

Evaluation

Students develop a presentation that answers the essential question(s).

The presentations should provide enough background so that classmates will gain an understanding of the topic even if they do not possess prior knowledge of it.

Students may present their information to the class in many ways, including:
- Flowcharts
- Multimedia presentations
- Web pages
- Summary tables
- Concept maps
- Venn diagrams
- Experiments and results

Provide students with a clear understanding of the grading criteria that will be used to evaluate their efforts.

Provide links to online rubrics that will allow students to know what grading criteria will be used. Following are examples that could be used for a variety of projects:

Include a phrase such as, "**Review the criteria for the rubric** on which your individual grade will be based."

OR

"You will also receive a collaborative grade. **Review the criteria** on which I will determine you collaborative grade."

Explain how the grades will be counted or averaged.

Writing Activity: Student evaluation of a CyberInquiry should reflect the following information:

Ask students if they had interpreted questions and information differently, how the outcome might have changed.

Ask students if they were flexible enough to compromise with the group and attain resolution, or if they yielded to group pressures.

Ask students what new questions the issue(s) generated. Why would these new questions be important in answering the original question(s)?

Exhibit Center

CyberInquiries provide a logical transition step from a Scavenger Hunt or Internet Discovery to a WebQuest. The examples in Exhibits 8.1, 8.2, and 8.3 illustrate the progression from the earlier, less complex activities to activities that are more sophisticated and challenging. Many of the examples that we have presented were first seen in the Guided Tour Exhibit Center *(see Chapter 4)*. Notice how the model builds as the teacher gathers more information.

The technical skills required to create a CyberInquiry build on those skills developed in creating a Guided Tour (copying and pasting), a Scavenger Hunt (search techniques), and Web pages (hyperlinks and tables). Many teachers who first view the CyberInquiry think that it might be too difficult to complete. However, teachers find that if they build from the Guided Tour to the CyberInquiry the task is much easier and less time-consuming.

Exhibit 8.1   *The 1960s: Contradictory Messages*

The 1960s: Contradictory Messages

http://www.spa3.k12.sc.us/Cyberinquiry/decadeCyberInquiry.htm

Teacher Overview
- Students will develop a pictorial history of a particular time period. As a team, students will brainstorm ways in which to gather the information. The Internet may be used, but other materials and books may be used as well.
- Ninth grade English/Language Arts and U.S. History
- The student will use writing to interpret, analyze, and evaluate the ideas of others.
- The student will use inferential and critical thinking to create written responses to a variety of texts across the curriculum.
- Have students collect information on the 1960s. What are the defining moments of the 1960s? Ask students to bring in pictures that grandparents/parents may have from the '60s. Bring in music from the decade.

Introduction
The 1960s has long been considered a decade of rebellion. One of the famous sayings from the time was "don't trust anyone over 30." From flower power to Vietnam protests, the '60s were contradictory. What made the 1960s so contradictory? Why were peace and love such com-

---

Exhibit 8.1 *The 1960s: Contradictory Messages (continued)*

mon themes? What are some of the important scenes from the decade? (Please remember that you must follow the rules of school Internet use. Material gathered must be appropriate for school. Please review the school Internet policy.)

As part of a Public Broadcasting series on the new millennium, you have been asked to produce an overview of the 1960s that explores the questions," "Why were the 1960s so contradictory?" and "Why were peace and love such common themes?" Your production is limited to 15 minutes. You have been given a notebook in which to document your data. Please remember, unless you are able to document where you received information, you will not be able to use it when the production is broadcast.

- Look at the task carefully. Divide the project into five different parts—a part for each team member. Brainstorm in your group and speculate about what you know and what you think you know. Why do you think there are so many contradictions about the 1960s? Each member of the group should jot down ideas in the notebook.
- Students may wish to use the KWHL template available in most graphic organizer programs.
- KWHL questions are: What do you know? What do you want to know? How will you find it out? What did you learn?
- Write some smaller questions that you might answer from the task. Make sure that you understand the questions.
- The team should divide the project into parts so that each team member researches one aspect of the assignment. After investigating background information, the group should reconvene to determine if any changes should be made in assignments.

Investigation
Explore the following Web sites. Be sure you document where you collect information.

Baby Boomer Headquarters: The Sixties Section
http://www.bbhq.com/sixties.htm
A very rich site that has links to music, trivia, and other baby boomer-type concerns.

Exhibit 8.1 *The 1960s: Contradictory Messages (continued)*

The Sixties
http://www.slip.net/~scmetro/1960s.htm
Collections of 1960s links and music. Transcripts of famous speeches are available.

The Astronauts and the Race to the Moon
http://www.1960s.net/space.htm
When Russia went into space first, the United States vowed to take over the lead and land a man on the moon.

The Psychedelic '60s
http://www.lib.virginia.edu/exhibits/1960s/index.html
This special collection from the University of Virginia features Woodstock, books, music, radical groups, civil rights, the Vietnam War, and arts from the 1960s.

The American Experience
http://www.pbs.org/wgbh/amex/vietnam/index.html
This Web site is a companion to the PBS series of the same name.

Vietnam: Yesterday and Today
http://servercc.oakton.edu/~wittman/
The site explores who and what Vietnam is and was to us. It also gives drama, novels, and poems of and about Vietnam.

Dr. Martin Luther King, Jr.
http://seattletimes.nwsource.com/mlk/movement/Seatimeline.html
The Seattle Times covers the civil rights movement through the eyes of Dr. King.

Webcorp Multimedia
http://www.webcorp.com/civilrights/index.htm
Audio clips from the 1960s are available.

After investigating the information, get together with your group to discuss any necessary revisions in your search strategy. Do you have an idea of material that you would like to research more thoroughly? Have you gotten too much information on one topic? What would be the most interesting information?

Exhibit 8.1 | *The 1960s: Contradictory Messages (continued)*

Gathering & Sorting

- Students should search for additional information on the Internet that relates to the part of the topic that they are researching. If students find something that might be useful to another team member, they should write down the URL for the team member.
- Remember to document where the information was found. PBS has very high standards for accuracy.
- Collect the following:

    Pictures of key political leaders

    Artifacts from fads

    A speech from a person who was alive during the decade

    A sample of the fashion of the time

    An audio recording or the words of a hit song

    A list of popular entertainment

    A list of popular sports

    A painting from the decade

    Three significant scientists or inventors of the time

    The most significant advance during this time in science or in the humanities

    Ten books published during this decade

    List three important businesses/industries during this period of time.

    What ten items were made during this decade?

    What war(s) or military conflicts were occurring?
- You have collected and read much information on the 1960s. What are some of the questions that you would like to explore further? How does the 1960s generation or the 1960s decade compare with your generation and your decade?

Portfolio

Please access the portfolio that your teacher has in the classroom.

- Review the materials that you have collected and determine what is the "best" information to add. Students should add one piece of information to this collection. You must decide the area and the information to leave.
- Attach an index card to the information that details your reason for adding the information to the portfolio. How does the information enrich the portfolio? Why is it important?

Exhibit 8.1 *The 1960s: Contradictory Messages (continued)*

- Students: Write a two- to three-page persuasive essay addressing the topic, "The most significant person to have lived during the 1960s was (select a person who in your judgment had the greatest impact on the 1960s)." Explore why he or she is the most significant person? Why does your person's activity have the greatest impact on the 1960s? How was he or she influential?
- Access the scoring rubric to see how you will be graded.

Sharing

- Meet in your group. Come to a consensus regarding what information should be presented in the multimedia presentation.
- The presentations should provide enough background so classmates will gain an understanding of the topic even if they do not possess prior knowledge of it.

Evaluation

Provide students with a clear understanding of the grading criteria that will be used to evaluate their efforts. Access the scoring rubric to see how you will be graded.

Before the presentation, each class member should read the essential questions and, in groups of five, develop rubrics. The following Web sites provide examples of rubrics that your group may consider.

http://edWeb.sdsu.edu/triton/july/rubrics/Rubric_Template.html
http://edWeb.sdsu.edu/triton/tidepoolunit/Rubrics/collrubric.html

Group members should complete a CyberInquiry evaluation that elicits comments on the assignment, questions, or concerns they had about the project.

>What did they like best?
>How did they approach the search?
>Why did they divide the topic as they did?
>How effective was their approach.
>What would they do differently?
>What worked well? Why?

Commentary: This CyberInquiry does a great job at spiraling the learning for students. Unlike the Guided Tour on the 1960s, which is rooted in knowledge- or fact-based questions, this activity challenges students to evaluate information, develop meaningful products, and write opinions based on sound research. The 1960s CyberInquiry is rooted in the essential questions: *"Why were peace and love such common themes?"* and *"Why were the 1960s so contradictory?"* It is quite clear that these are questions that students will be forced to wrestle with before they can resolve them in their minds. Employing sound instructional strategy, the teacher provides some directions to write down everything students think they know or don't know about the period. In turn, the students will be prepared to write effective questions to help them understand the task as well as to determine how to divide the different parts of the project. During the gathering and sorting of information, students will come across tons of valuable information and are encouraged to write down questions that they may wish to explore further.

Exhibit 8.2 | *John Glenn–Up in Space*

John Glenn—Up in Space

http://www.spa3.k12.sc.us/cyberinquiry/glenn/upinspace.htm

Teacher Overview
- Students will research pre-selected Internet sites, as well as those that they have researched and that have met teacher approval. As a group, students will consider serious ethical, moral, and scientific issues surrounding space travel and the elderly.
- **Ninth Grade Global Studies/World Geography**
  - 10.8.5. Develop strategies to respond to constraints placed on human systems by the physical environment

Introduction
Space flight has long been the source of national pride and curiosity in the United States. Until the late 1980s, the former Soviet Union and the United States competed with one another to see which one could achieve the next great accomplishment in the world of space travel.

In November 1998, Senator and former astronaut John Glenn became the oldest person to travel into outer space. Not only was Senator Glenn's mission an important milestone for space travel, but it also raised serious ethical questions. Years of scientific research have uncovered that the human body undergoes significant transformation and stress while subjected to a zero-gravity environment. This is especially significant for the elderly.

Exhibit 8.2 *John Glenn–Up in Space (continued)*

You have been asked to appear before a special Senate committee that is investigating whether or not the government should fund any future space travel that involves elderly astronauts. In a written report, please address the following questions:

Are there any viable alternatives or solutions that would allow important scientific research to continue in space without endangering the well-being of elderly astronauts?

What have been some of the scientific advancements associated with space travel so far? Are they significant?

How could society benefit from studying the effects of space travel on the elderly?

Overall, what are some of the benefits of exploring space?

You need to address this important question: "Despite the potential advances in medicine, should the elderly be allowed/encouraged to participate in space flights which researchers speculate are harmful to the human biological systems, especially in the elderly?"

Look at the task carefully. Divide the project into five different parts—a part for each team member. Brainstorm in your group and speculate about what you know, and what you think you know. Please keep detailed notes in your projects notebook.

Write some smaller questions that you might answer from the task. Make sure that you understand the questions.

The team should divide the project into parts so that each team member researches one aspect of the assignment. After investigating background information, the group should reconvene to determine if any changes should be made in assignments.

Investigation
Explore the following Web sites. Be sure you document where you collect information.

Exhibit 8.2 *John Glenn–Up in Space (continued)*

The Astronauts and the Race to the Moon
http://www.1960s.net/space.htm
When Russia went into space first, the United States vowed to take over the lead and land a man on the moon.

Database of U.S. Astronauts and Soviet Cosmonauts
http://www.jsc.nasa.gov/bios/more.html
This site provides a searchable biographical database of former and current U.S. astronauts and Soviet cosmonauts. Additionally, included is a new section comparing life on earth with life on a space shuttle.

Space.com
http://www.space.com/
General space information site with search features available.

After investigating the information, get together with your group to discuss any necessary revisions in your search strategy. Do you have an idea of material that you would like to research more thoroughly? Have you gotten too much information on one topic? What would be the most interesting of the information?

Gathering & Sorting
Students should search for additional information that relates to the part of the topic that they are researching. If you find something that might be useful to another team member, write down the URL for the team member.

Remember, you need to document where you gather information.
Collect the following:

- Pictures of famous astronauts
- Diagrams and illustrations that show the effects of space travel on the human body
- Direct quotes from astronauts and other experts in the field of space travel
- A sample of equipment used by astronauts on a mission
- Cost estimates for funding space shuttle missions

You have collected and read much information on the effects of space travel on the human body. What are some of the questions that you would like to explore further?

Exhibit 8.2 *John Glenn–Up in Space* (*continued*)

Portfolio

Please access the portfolio that your teacher has in the classroom.

Review the materials that you have collected and determine what is the "best" information to add. Students should add one piece of information to this collection. You must decide the area and the information to leave.

Attach an index card to the information that details your reason for adding the information to the portfolio. How does the information enrich the portfolio? Why is it important?

Students: Write a two- to three-page persuasive essay addressing the task assigned: *Despite the potential advances in medicine, should the elderly be allowed/encouraged to participate in space flights, which researchers know are harmful to the human biological systems, especially in the elderly?*

Access the scoring rubric to see how you will be graded.

Sharing

Meet in your group. Come to a consensus regarding what information should be presented in the multimedia presentation.

The presentations should provide enough background so classmates will gain an understanding of the topic even if they do not possess prior knowledge of it.

Evaluation

Provide students with a clear understanding of the grading criteria that will be used to evaluate their efforts. Access the scoring rubric to see how you will be graded.

Before the presentation, each class members should read the essential questions and, in groups of five, develop rubrics. The following sites offer examples that your group may consider.

http://edWeb.sdsu.edu/triton/july/rubrics/Rubric_Template.html
http://edWeb.sdsu.edu/triton/tidepoolunit/Rubrics/collrubric.html

Exhibit 8.2 *John Glenn–Up in Space (continued)*

Group members should complete a CyberInquiry evaluation that elicits comments on the assignment, questions, or concerns they had about the project. What did they like best? How did they approach the search? Why did they divide the topic as they did? How effective was their approach? What would they do differently? What worked well? Why?

Commentary: The **Up in Space** CyberInquiry focuses more intently on the moral and ethical issues surrounding the essential question: *"Despite the potential advances in medicine, should the elderly be allowed/encouraged to participate in space flights, which researchers speculate are harmful to the human biological systems, especially in the elderly?"* The teacher begins with an interesting, timely overview that is vital to "hooking" the students into eagerly approaching this assignment. In this scenario, the students are informed that they will be presenting their recommendations to a special committee that is pondering this important question.

It is important that the essential question be tied to a concrete task. This way, students will begin to make connections between reasoning and questioning and real-world application. The intent of the essential question is to lead students into answering the concrete question: *"Should the government fund future space travel that involves elderly astronauts?"* Now, cost is looked at in two areas: the cost to human health and the fiscal cost of sending astronauts into space. This kind of activity could very easily be modified into a WebQuest. With an issue such as this one that looks at so many debatable questions concerning age, money, and government, roles could quickly be developed to explore these questions on an even higher level.

Anne Frank and the Children of the Holocaust: Who Were the Heroes?

Adapted from a WebQuest by Jim Heffner, Polly Hembree, and Alicia Womick

http://www.spa3.k12.sc.us/cyberinquiry/annefrank/heroinquiry.htm

Teacher Overview

Objective
- The student will explore the question of courage and the heroic spirit of Anne Frank and other people in the Holocaust.

Curriculum Standards
- Middle School Studies:
  - Describe the causes and course of World War II, including the Holocaust, the character of the war at home and abroad, and its reshaping of the United States' role in world affairs.
- Middle School English:
  - The student will identify universal themes in the literature of all cultures and relate to personal experience.
  - The student will analyze and evaluate formal presentations.
    - Critique relationships among purpose, audience, and content of presentations.
    - Critique effectiveness of presentations.
  - The student will compose in a variety of genres and evaluate for effectiveness.
    - Evaluate information from text and utilize in own writings.
    - Support alternative point of view from text.
    - Establish pros/cons of chosen stance.

Materials: paper, pencil, and Internet

Time: Three days

Description: As though they are journalists preparing a documentary on heroism for CBS, the students will research information about the courage of Anne Frank and other children of the Holocaust. Classmates will answer questions, make judgments as to what pictures and data to include, and write some journal responses to include in a possible question-and-answer period.

Introduction

"Over one million children under the age of 16 died in the Holocaust: Anne Frank was one of them."

You have just been hired to help create a documentary on heroism. You will utilize information about Anne Frank and the children of the Holocaust as you explore this topic for network television. Your job is to research information about Anne Frank and other children of the Holocaust.

The important question that you must answer is "Who were the heroes?" How do you define "hero"? Were these children in Anne Frank's diary heroes?" Are other people the heroes in Anne's diary? Why?

You are to complete each activity or activities assigned by your teacher and follow the instructions that are given. Good Luck!

Before beginning your search, you may want to review information about the Holocaust.

Investigation

The investigation is structured as a Jigsaw. Each person in a group will select a particular aspect of the topic to research from the five tasks listed. Preview the various tasks and decide which person will be assigned to each task. Remember that you will be presenting your information to the rest of the group, so keep good notes.

Activity # 1

You are going to take a virtual visit to Germany in the year 1943. You will visit the following Web sites to see some faces of the people and scenes related to the Holocaust. Read any data related to the photographs.

Anne Frank's Story in Pictures
http://www.annefrank.com/

French Children of the Holocaust
http://www.dialnsa.edu/Klarsfeld/children.html

Picture Tour
http://remember.org/jacobs/index.html

Write a journal response to the photographs and information given.
Describe your emotions and thoughts.

Which photographs would you choose for the documentary and why? Be
sure to give the Web site address and name of the photograph.

Activity #2
You are now going to choose some musical selections for our documentary. Explore the following sites to find musical pieces you may want to
use. Choose a musical piece that you think could be the theme song or an
instrumental for the documentary. Give your reasons for choosing this
work.

http://www.zamir.org/resources/holocaust.html
This site contains listings of books, articles, annotated musical selections,
selected recordings, and musical compositions.

http://www.english.upenn.edu/~afilreis/Holocaust/phila-orchestra.
html
This site contains details of Terezin, a Nazi concentration camp. Prisoners
were allowed to compose and perform music.

Activity #3
Read the literature about the children of the Holocaust. Select works that
especially express the courage and heroic spirit of the children. After
selecting three works, print each and explain how these particular works
reflect courage.

Anne Frank's Diary...Selected Entries
http://www.annefrank.com/site/af_life/2_life_exrpt/2_life_diary.htm

Poem "Daniel"
http://www.mtsu.edu/~baustin/daniel.html

Stories of Survivors
http://spidey.sfusd.k12.ca.us/schwww/sch773/review/ngo.html
http://spidey.sfusd.k12.ca.us/schwww/sch773/review/manzano.html

Child Survivor's Testimony on Video with Audio
http://www.library.yale.edu/testimonies/

Activity # 4
Anne Frank's diary has been translated into many languages. Millions of students read Anne's diary each year. One of the people who assisted Anne and the others in hiding was Miep Gies. Pretend that Miep Gies will be a guest speaker on the TV documentary. Read the information concerning Anne's life and her diary. Also read Miep's comments about Anne. Prepare questions to ask Miep Gies about the heroic Anne.

Information About Anne's Diary (e.g., publication, authenticity)
http://www.annefrank.com

Anne Frank's House with related information
http://www.annefrank.nl/eng/default2.html

Activity #5
In this activity you will view children's art about the Holocaust. Pretend that you will invite the child artists to the show. Choose three art works from the selections. Write a journal response for each work. Explain why each work best depicts the courage of the children of the Holocaust.

http://remember.org/imagine/imagine1.html

After each person has investigated the information, convene the group. Present the information that each person has gathered to the group. Do you have enough information? Are there any necessary revisions in your search strategy? Do you have an idea of material that you would like to research more thoroughly? Have you gotten too much information on one topic? What part of the information collected is most promising for determining who were the heroes?

Gathering & Sorting

- Students should search for additional information that relates to the part of the topic that they are researching. If you find something that might be useful to another team member, write down the URL for the team member.
- Remember, you need to document where you gather information.
- Collect the following:
  - Pictures of Anne Frank and other children of the Holocaust
  - Diagrams and illustrations of Anne's living quarters during the war
  - Direct quotes from Holocaust survivors as well as quotes from survivors of World War II
  - Excerpts from Anne Frank's diary
  - Statistics on the number of people killed during World War II broken down by category (i.e., number killed in battle, civilian casualties, famine, and the Holocaust)

You have collected and read much information about the Holocaust. What are some of the questions that you would like to explore further?

Portfolio

Please access the portfolio that your teacher has in the classroom.

- Review the materials that you have collected and determine what is the "best" information to add. Students should add one piece of information to this collection. You must decide the area and the information to leave.
- Attach an index card to the information that details your reason for adding the information to the portfolio. How does the information enrich the portfolio? Why is it important?
- Access the scoring rubric to see how you will be graded.

Sharing

- Meet in your group. Come to a consensus as to what information should be presented in the multimedia presentation.
- The presentations should provide enough background so classmates will gain an understanding of the topic even if they do not possess prior knowledge of it.

Evaluation

Provide students with a clear understanding of the grading criteria that will be used to evaluate their efforts. Access the scoring rubric to see how you will be graded.

Before the presentation, each class member should read the essential questions and, in groups of five, develop rubrics. The following Web sites offer examples that your group may consider.

http://edWeb.sdsu.edu/triton/july/rubrics/Rubric_Template.html
http://edWeb.sdsu.edu/triton/tidepoolunit/Rubrics/collrubric.html

Group members should complete a CyberInquiry evaluation that elicits comments on the assignment, questions, or concerns they had about the project. What did they like best? How did they approach the search? Why did they divide the topic as they did? How effective was their approach? What would they do differently? What worked well? Why?

Commentary: The Anne Frank CyberInquiry goes deep to the heart of writing good essential questions. This activity looks at two of the most fascinating characteristics of human nature—heroism and courage. Because today's society often sets very different standards for heroism, this activity requires students to evaluate this concept from a unique and unfamiliar perspective. Forcing students to consider questions that are outside of their limited schemas will help move them toward higher-level thinking. The teachers masterfully tie the students into the activity by personalizing it with a poignant quote: *"Over one million children under the age of 16 died in the Holocaust: Anne Frank was one of them."*

Technical Corner

For technical assistance with the topics discussed in this chapter, please refer to the Appendix.

Skill	Description	Appendix Page Number
Chapter 8 Technical Corner		
Multi-Tasking	Multi-tasking involves simultaneously running multiple software programs and switching between them to perform a variety of functions. This skill is essential when developing Web-based learning activities.	197

Chapter 9

Transforming Learning: The WebQuest

"You can observe a lot by watching."
— *Yogi Berra*

A more sophisticated use of Web-based instruction is the development of a WebQuest—one the most fascinating applications on the Web. A WebQuest builds upon the skills and knowledge learned with Guided Tours, Scavenger Hunts, and CyberInquiries. Hotlists or resource sites used for the other models become the foundation for developing a WebQuest.

After being exposed to a variety of information collected from the Web and other sources, students are asked to interpret and analyze the information, and to prepare a report on the information for a particular audience or a particular purpose. By manipulating the data, the information is transformed. The chief characteristic of a WebQuest is the roles that students assume. Gathering information to support conflicting points of view, the students assume the role of advocate for a particular position.

WebQuests, which originated from the innovative work of Bernie Dodge and Tom March, transform the way we looked at the Web. Developed in 1995, the WebQuest model that Bernie Dodge created moved us beyond the "look at these neat sites" phase and fired our imagination.

The World Wide Web became more than a repository for extraneous information. It became a place to conduct an adventure, a simulation, and an exciting discovery. Suddenly we saw that the Web would change what hadn't been changed in a hundred years—the look of the school classroom. Those who dream envisioned students—in secondary as well as elementary schools—working in small groups, moving to learning centers, and constructing their own learning through simulations and demonstrations.

Student-centered and inquiry-based, a WebQuest challenges students to explore the Web. Most WebQuests include the links that are appropriate for students to research as well as suggestions for further research. WebQuests are generally constructed around a scenario of interest to students. Traditionally, WebQuests have an introduction, a process, a task, a list of resources, a conclusion, and an evaluation.

Asking teachers to develop a WebQuest before they have had an opportunity to master the earlier stages of the Web-based learning framework often results in frustration. However, once teachers believe that they can handle the technical and instructional aspects of a WebQuest, they tend to develop outstanding activities.

Process Step 6: WebQuest

In a WebQuest, there are traditionally six steps: **introduction, quest, process, resources, evaluation**, and **conclusion**. As part of the process, students each take a role, often one that will produce dissonance or opposing points of view. As part of the conclusion, students, playing their respective roles, reach a consensus on the topic.

The idea of establishing roles that conflict with each other is somewhat of an anathema to many classroom teachers. Even though the world around us swirls in chaos and conflict, the idea of promoting this reality in a classroom activity causes discomfort for teachers.

The unique challenge facing teachers who choose to do WebQuests with their students is that the teacher must become very familiar with many sides and opinions surrounding a debatable issue. For many teachers with two, three, or four preps, investing the time to investigate and understand all the different sides is problematic.

Teachers point out that students have a difficult time working with roles. Students may not be capable of internalizing a role assigned to them. They may also have trouble viewing that role within the big picture of the other conflicting roles an essential question may involve. A student's frame of reference is less developed than ours. For the middle school student, for example, family and peers often shape opinion.

Creating a WebQuest

Before developing a WebQuest, a teacher must determine the unit of study, the essential question, and the academic standards covered by the Quest. Because they are interdisciplinary, WebQuests require cross-subject teaming. In order to create the dissonance of the roles, multiple perspectives need to be developed—whether they are the scientist, the ethicist, or the mayor of a town. A media specialist is an ideal addition to the team because media specialists tend to see topics and themes from a multidisciplinary perspective. In addition, as students collect information and develop perspectives, they need to be knowledgeable about copyright laws and about citing sources.

Many of the decisions are made prior to the actual development of a WebQuest. We encourage interdisciplinary teams of teachers to develop a Guided Tour or a Scavenger Hunt first, gradually refining ideas and the essential question as they begin the collection of Web sites related to the unit.

From the teacher notes or overview, the actual development of the WebQuest begins with an **introduction**. The introduction is the scenario that hooks students into a real-world problem. Within the introduction, background information and Web sites are provided for all students to review and to read. It is important that students have a common background, or that they have key information to get the "big picture." The key element of the introduction is generating interest and excitement among students. The WebQuest journey should be one that they want to take.

The second key part of the WebQuest is the **task**, or as Tom March calls it, "the Quest." Within the task, the teacher provides guiding questions that scaffold the information and the learning necessary to explore the essential question. The task that students must accomplish and its importance are spelled out. Various roles that a student may assume are described. Each role carries with it the potential for generating tension or dissonance and has additional information to explore that is tailored to that role. As a consequence, a group of students will have common background information as well as specialized information that prepares them for their role.

A WebQuest is a collaborative work for students; however, some teachers are uncomfortable with assigning group grades alone. Through the development of the roles, a teacher may assign individual grades as well since students will work individually in gathering, processing, and reacting to information.

The third step is the **process**. In this step, the teacher outlines the method that the students will use in pursuing the research. At this juncture, the teachers clarify whether each student will pursue the research independently or whether they should compare ideas along the way.

The key aspect of the process is to outline the procedures the students should follow in completing the group work. Consensus documents and presentations are among the possible products that the teacher may stipulate that the group should produces.

The fourth step involves **resources**. In addition to the collected Web sites, the teacher specifies what other information may be available on the topic. It may be the work of another group that previously completed the WebQuest or articles and books from the media center.

The fifth step entails the **evaluation and conclusion**. These are listed together because they are dependent upon one another. As with all well-designed group projects, the evaluation will include a rubric that establishes grading criteria for group and individual work. The teacher should stipulate how these grades will be averaged or counted for a final grade.

The conclusion is important because it is where students reflect on the WebQuest. Were they successful? Why? What could have led them to be more successful? Did they compromise or did they yield to group pressure? Perhaps the most important questions of all for developing high-quality units are "What new questions did the issues generate?" and "What additional roles or replacement roles are needed for the WebQuests?"

The conceptual framework for the WebQuest shows the complexity of the learning model.

WebQuest Conceptual Framework

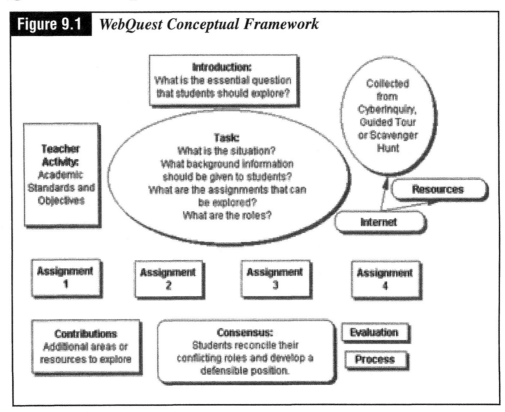

Figure 9.1 *WebQuest Conceptual Framework*

This diagram was created using Inspiration® by Inspiration Software, Inc.

The WebQuest incorporates essential questions, has roles that often conflict, and provides real-world problems for students to solve. The beauty of the model lies in the fact that WebQuests may be used repeatedly, and different results and resolutions will result. That fact underscores the transformational power of the WebQuest.

The roles provide the sandpaper that refines student ideas. Information is safe and secure until it is questioned. Once information is questioned, we must go back, revisit, review, and restate—the beginnings of transformation. We transform information when we begin to use it in a new way, when we begin to manipulate it. The use of the roles in a WebQuest provides the opportunity for students to learn new information that is central to their role, and then to attempt to sway other students who have internalized different viewpoints.

Initially, students relentlessly hang on to their viewpoints. During the early stages of using WebQuest, we often see the "bully" or the student with the dominant personality prevailing. As students become savvier in the art of discussion and consensus, they exercise more care in reaching conclusions.

As part of our professional development, we have developed a WebQuest rubric. The rubric can be used for self-evaluation as teachers develop their own WebQuest. The rubric is a ruler; it allows us to measure how closely what we develop is to being a WebQuest. Before teachers create a WebQuest, we ask them to be analytical in identifying WebQuests. For that purpose, the rubric was developed as a means to evaluate WebQuests.

WebQuest Evaluation Form

	Proficient	Competent	Basic
Frames the essential question	The essential question scaffolds learning, spanning Bloom's Taxonomy; the learner is encouraged to wonder; the learner is encouraged to invent his or her own solution; the essential question builds on prior knowledge.	The question spans the lower levels of Bloom's Taxonomy—knowledge, comprehension, and application; the student is able to quickly reach a conclusion in response to the question; does not attempt to have students make judgments or evaluate.	The question can be answered directly; the focus of the question is knowledge and comprehension; the question has one obvious answer (i.e., Is slavery good or bad?).
Connects WebQuest to academic standards at developmentally appropriate grade level	WebQuest is interdisciplinary with clearly targeted standards; standards are directly correlated to the tasks.	WebQuest is not interdisciplinary; no effort is made to connect to other disciplines; standards are related to the WebQuest.	WebQuest lists multiple items from standards that are peripherally connected to the topic; standards listed are not appropriate to the WebQuest.
Engaging scenario & tasks	The scenario and task is engaging for students; the task provides sufficient background information to excite the interest of students; the procedures are clearly outlined.	The scenario is interesting; the tasks are not clearly defined; inadequate background information is supplied for each role; directions are clear.	The scenario is one-dimensional; the task requires a student to research at the knowledge or comprehension level; directions are vague.
Relevant Internet sources at appropriate grade level for students	All information listed is relevant information; sources are differentiated for each role; puts meaning of the problem in personal, social, or community perspectives; sources are at an appropriate reading level for students.	Information listed includes relevant and irrelevant materials; uses a limited number of sources; sites do not encourage reflection; sites may be developmentally inappropriate.	Links to sites and materials are not directly connected to the assignment; uses one source; interprets meaning from one source; does not provide information for students to analyze or interpret.
Roles are interesting and create dissonance	The WebQuest introduces characters who would interact with the information in the "real world;" there are several characters; the characters are unique; characters have different points of view on the subject.	The characters are similar in belief or thought; there is insufficient background information; there are two or fewer roles; the character is clearly "invented" and would not be involved in the scenario in the real world.	There are no clearly defined characters; characters are stereotypical or one-dimensional; background information is the same for all characters; there is one role in the WebQuest.

WebQuest Evaluation Form (continued)

	Proficient	**Competent**	**Basic**
Produces product connected to assignment	The description of the product is clearly and coherently presented; product is clearly related to task; product is unique and would clearly stretch the group's thinking.	The product does not encourage students to reflect and evaluate contrasting points of view; product is similar to other products that have been produced.	Product is not clearly connected to the question.
Creativity	Student would be able to generate multiple approaches of looking at the problem; student would be challenged to demonstrate different approaches.	Student would be able to demonstrate one clear approach to understanding the problem; does not ask students to draw conclusion.	Student copies and pastes from the Internet without discrimination; product demonstrates little connection to the question; product does not show reflection.

The World Wide Web offers many wonderful templates that can help teachers create WebQuests. Explore Web'n Flow **<http://www. ozline.com>**, Filamentality **<http://www.kn.pacbell.com/wired/fil/>**, or the Kiko WebQuest site **<http://www.kiko.com/wqst/index.jsp>**.

We also have created our own form. The WebQuest Template that follows is posted at **<http://www.spa3.k12.sc.us/WebQuestTemplate/ Webquesttemp.htm>**.

We advise teachers to save the template as an MS Word document. The template may then be edited. As teachers begin to use the model, they are usually dependent upon the template. After successfully using the template once or twice, teachers generally become confident enough to venture out on their own.

WebQuest Template

Put the Title of the WebQuest Here

Developed by (put your name, an e-mail link, and your URL)

Overview
Describe what the lesson is about.

Specify content area (e.g., mathematics, language arts) and grade level (e.g., middle, elementary, early childhood).

Specify strands and objectives from the South Carolina Curriculum Standards that this WebQuest supports. List by subject area. (WebQuests should be interdisciplinary projects.)

List any special resources that a teacher would need in the classroom or in the media center for the students to complete the activity. For example, print resources in the media center, art reproductions, or video and audio materials.

Introduction
Write an introduction to your WebQuest that will give students some background about your topic. Try to interest them.

If your WebQuest is about a place, include some general information, a picture, and/or audio files.

If it is about a person, describe something about the person that gives general background to the students.

If you are creating a scenario with opposing points of view, describe the views briefly.

Remember, you want to interest the students in pursuing this WebQuest.

Quest(ions) and the Task
What are the guiding questions that students need to keep in mind in order to accomplish their task?

What is the task that the student(s) must undertake?

Why is the job necessary?

What are the circumstances surrounding the task or the question that may cause conflict?

What led up to this circumstance?

Is there more than one way of looking at this?

Can you see conflicting roles for people—such as environmentalist and industrialist?

You should briefly outline for student(s) what they are expected to learn. For example: Despite the known risks of space flight, should the elderly be encouraged to make space shuttle flights for the sake of gaining potentially beneficial medical knowledge?

Assign various roles to students. A good WebQuest generates some tension or conflict that must be resolved so you should try to develop two to four roles.

Remember, this should be a collaborative activity for students.

Roles

Role 1-
Role 2-
Role 3-
Role 4-

Process

Explain that students who have similar roles may work together to compare ideas based on the factual information they have collected, or that students may continue to pursue their role individually until the conflict generated by the original guiding question(s) forces them to resolve the issue with the entire group.

Once students have understood their roles and investigated the background material necessary to make informed decisions, then it is time for them to come together as a group to discuss the issue(s). Group work should result in a consensus document or presentation.

Give students directions on this group work.

Be sure that they understand that their role may place them in conflict with another person's role.

How should they resolve this conflict?

What overall idea should they keep in mind that will allow them to compromise?

Is there a greater good?

Provide options for how students may present their information to the group. Here are some ideas:

- Flowcharts
- Multimedia presentations
- Web pages
- Summary tables
- Concept maps
- Venn diagrams

Resources

Identify for the students which other resources they may use to complete their task(s).

Other resources may include:

PowerPoint software to develop an informative slideshow

Any URL links provided in this section

Classroom encyclopedias

Color printer

Periodicals from the media center

Evaluation

Provide students with a clear understanding of the grading criteria that will be used to evaluate their efforts.

Provide links to online rubrics that will allow students to know up front what grading criteria will be used. Following are examples that could be used for a variety of projects.

> Include a phrase such as, "Please review the criteria on which your individual grade will be based."
>
> OR
>
> "You will also receive a collaborative grade. Please review the criteria which will determine your collaborative grade."

Explain how the grades will be counted or averaged.

Conclusion

Explain to students how the conclusion will offer the opportunity to engage in further analysis. For example:

Ask students how their roles could have been interpreted in a different light.

Ask students if they had interpreted their roles differently, how the outcome might have changed.

Ask students if they were flexible enough to compromise with the group and attain resolution, or if they yielded to group pressures.

Ask students what new questions the issue(s) generated. Why would these new questions be important in answering the original question(s)?

Exhibit Center

What do the plights of the South American rainforests and the Northern Spotted Owl have in common? From an academic standpoint, both issues deal with destruction of natural habitat and wildlife. Both also deal with the costs and benefits of industry growth and economic expansion. For teachers with whom we work, the common theme of these issues is Earth Day. During the past two years, several teachers from different schools, who teach different subjects, came together to create WebQuests on topics that would help students learn about the importance of Earth Day.

In the following group of exhibits, we have included examples of a wide range of WebQuests. These activities challenge students to critically analyze information from opposing viewpoints. To successfully complete a WebQuest, students are required to raise their thinking to the highest levels of Bloom's Taxonomy.

Unlike the CyberInquiry in which students complete a task common to the group, the WebQuest requires students to become experts in their role and to logically defend a position on a debatable issue. The teacher takes on the role of facilitator and moderates any activities between groups that require reconciliation and consensus building.

Again, the following examples illustrate a wide variety of styles and difficulty levels. These WebQuests were developed with little beginning knowledge of creating Web pages and for the most part were created by novice computer users.

Exhibit 9.1 | *The Fate of the Rain Forests*

The Fate of the Rain Forests

Developed by Debbie Bullock, Janice Griffin, and Pamela King

http://www.spa3.k12.sc.us/WebQuests/Rainforests/index.htm

Introduction

Picture yourself in a beautiful, green forest, surrounded by thousands of tall trees. A brown spider monkey laughs at you as he swings from tree to tree. You reach out and pick a ripe mango. You close your eyes as you bite into the sweet, juicy fruit. You hear a cracking sound behind you and turn to see a bright red-and-blue parrot break a nut in his beak and peck out the fleshy meat. A pale pink orchid grows on the bark of the tree beside you. As you lean down to smell the fragrant flower, a green tree frog stares up at you with wide eyes, as he clings to the bark with his orange webbed feet. Suddenly the sky darkens, and it begins to rain. You reach out and pluck a huge leaf from a bush and hold it over your head for an umbrella. The cool rain falls on the surface of the waxy leaf and drips off the tip. As you begin walking to the shelter of your hut, a red-and-black king snake slithers across your path. No, this is not an imaginary place. It is a tropical rain forest. Tropical rain forests have existed for millions of years.

Overview

This lesson is about the challenges for the survival of the rain forests.

This unit is designed for upper elementary and is appropriate for use by science, social studies, and math teachers.

Exhibit 9.1 *The Fate of the Rain Forests (continued)*

In addition to Web sites included in this unit, a bibliography is located at the end of this project listing print, audio, and video resources. Go to **http://www.spa3.k12.sc.us/WebQuests/Rainforests/ StandardsBullock.htm** for specific strands and objectives from the South Carolina Curriculum Standards that are addressed in this WebQuest.

Introduction

Welcome to the world of the tropical rain forest, which is teeming with rare species of animals and plants that exist nowhere else on earth. Located between the Tropics of Cancer and Capricorn, rain forests are characterized by hot, humid weather all year long, which creates an environment conducive to an abundance of growth.

Hundreds of years ago, tropical rain forests encircled the globe, much like long, green arms, hugging the equator and covering 20 percent of the earth's land surface. Reduced to a mere 6 percent, the diminishing rain forest shelters more than half of all the plant and animal species living in the world today. Rapid deforestation has endangered the splendor of this tropical paradise.

Today's changing world has created new challenges for the survival of the rain forests. New forces, man-made, are in conflict with each other and with the existence of the rain forests. This conflict becomes important as people gain awareness that changes in one area of the world have an impact on all areas of the world. There are several points of view regarding how to best manage the rain forest. For example:

The **local government agencies** are concerned with the economic development of their countries.

The **logging industries** need wood for lumber and paper products.

The **medical community** relies heavily on the plants and insects of the rain forest.

The **indigenous peoples** are being affected by the changes and, at the same time, are causing some of the changes.

The **environmentalists** are concerned with the long-term impacts of deforestation.

Exhibit 9.1 *The Fate of the Rain Forests (continued)*

You will complete research into the activities of each of these groups—all having a stake in the survival of the rain forests.

Quest(ions) and the Task

Following are Web sites that provide information on many aspects of the rain forest. Before you begin your investigation, take time to define words you may be seeing for the first time at **http://www.spa3.k12.sc.us/ WebQuests/Rainforests/VocabularyWords.htm.**

Government Officials, Economic Conditions
http://forests.org/ric/wrr_top_ten/welcome.htm (click on "Background")

http://forests.org/

http://www.geocities.com/yosemite/trails/1039/

http://www.rainforestfoundationuk.org/rainhome.html

What are the economic conditions of most of the countries that encompass rain forests? What is the state of their industries? What is the standard of living for the average citizen?

What steps are the government officials allowing or encouraging that are destroying the rain forests?

Logging Officials
http://www.geocities.com/Yosemite/Trails/1039/

What is the demand for wood from the rain forests? Is it available elsewhere? If so, is there a reason to obtain it from rain forests over other sources? Is there a policy in place for renewal of forest products? (What kind of wood is available from rain forests? What is the reason for the popularity of this kind of wood?)

Medical Profession
http://www.ran.org/ran/index.html (Rainforest Information box, Fact Sheet, Basic Rainforest Information, Facts About the Rainforest, 5F Medicinal.)

Exhibit 9.1 *The Fate of the Rain Forests (continued)*

http://rain-tree.com/

What are some of the products that are obtained from the rain forests? Are these available in any other location in the world? Why is there such interest in preserving the rain forest by medical researchers?

Environmentalists
http://www.bagheera.com/inthewild/spotlight.htm

What is deforestation? What are some of the effects of deforestation on the rain forest?

Describe to what extent deforestation is occurring in the world's rain forest. What actions can environmentalists take to protect the rain forest?

Indigenous People
http://www.eduWeb.com/agriculture/ag1.html

http://www.geocities.com/Yosemite/Trails/1039

Who are some of the indigenous people of tropical rain forests? Describe their cultures?

Describe the impact on the indigenous people of the deforestation of the rain forest.

What part, if any, have these people played in the deforestation of the tropical rain forests? Why do you think they have made the decisions they have?

Process
Consider the roles listed in the preceding section. Visit the Web resources listed beneath the role you are assigned. During the first week of this WebQuest, write answers to the questions that are given with each site. See also additional resources at **http://www.spa3.k12.sc.us/WebQuests/ Rainforests/RainforestResources.html.**

Keep a log of the facts you discover and note the source.

During Week Two, develop a 10-minute persuasive presentation to convince your classmates that your activities are justified. Introduce yourself in the role you have researched. Throughout the presentation, remember

Exhibit 9.1 *The Fate of the Rain Forests (continued)*

you ARE that person and you should present yourself in a believable manner. Present your information in a way that will capture the interest of your classmates. Some suggested techniques are posters, charts, maps, graphs, props, audiovisuals, and computer presentations.

With the teacher as the moderator, all students involved in this WebQuest will brainstorm solutions and reach a consensus as to the fate of the rain forests. **A management policy will be drafted.** Copies will be mailed to organizations that students identify as making policy in managing the rain forests.

Resources
Please visit **http://www.spa3.k12.sc.us/WebQuests/Rainforests/ RainforestResources.html** to see a list of additional resources.

Evaluation
Please visit **http://www.spa3.k12.sc.us/WebQuests/Rainforests/ rubric.htm** to review the criteria on which your individual grade will be based. Note that this includes a collaborative grade.

Conclusion
In the web of life, we are all connected. With a lack of a cooperative effort—and with many factions considering only their needs—we are jeopardizing the world's greatest storehouse of biological resources and one of the planet's critical climate control systems. It is only through development of a thoughtful, coordinated policy of management that the fate of the rain forest will be a positive one.

Commentary: When a group of teachers taking our professional development class expressed interest in creating a WebQuest that tied in directly to Earth Day, we were all quite excited. Earth Day is widely promoted in our district, and teachers and students work hard to make the day rewarding and educational. The "rain forest group," as they came to be known, consisted of two elementary school teachers, a media specialist, and a guidance counselor. What amazed us about them was not only the fine quality work that they accomplished but also the teamwork and collaboration that they displayed.

As can be imagined, the "rain forest group" had somewhat of a multiple personality. With two different grade-level teachers, a media specialist, and a guidance counselor, good communication skills were going to be vital to achieving success. The dynamics that unfolded were interesting. Without outside suggestions, the group naturally divided the work by who was better at each particular task. For example, the grade-level teachers were more familiar with the destruction of the rain forests and were able to guide the group toward developing a good essential question. The media specialist was more comfortable with technology than the others, and she was responsible for general technical issues and for things like adding graphics and hyper-links. The guidance counselor showed a great deal of skill using search engines and was responsible for guiding the searches for information.

Exhibit 9.2 *The Love Canal Debate*

The Love Canal Debate

Developed by Caroline Davis, Donna Kennedy, Marcia Phillips, Shelly Sawyer, and Debbie Taylor

http://www.spa3.k12.sc.us/WebQuests/LoveCanal/index.htm

Overview
This WebQuest is about a situation involving the dumping of hazardous wastes at Love Canal, New York. This is an interdisciplinary activity, which includes social studies, science, and language arts. The activity is appropriate for upper elementary school through high school.

Introduction
Love Canal, New York began in 1892 when William T. Love proposed digging a canal to connect the upper and lower parts of the Niagara River. The canal was never completed. However, from 1920-1953, the canal was used to dump hazardous wastes. Read about hazardous wastes at **http://www.spa3.k12.sc.us/WebQuests/LoveCanal/definition.htm**.

In 1953, the canal area was covered with dirt and presumed safe. When area residents started reporting health problems, officials began to inves-tigate the dumping of the hazardous wastes. They decided that Love Canal was a health hazard and evacuated the area. Since that time, a Superfund organization has been set up to clean up the waste site. As a result, in the early 1990s, people began moving back into Love Canal. Many of the homes have been renovated and resold to new citizens at much lower rates than in other surrounding communities. People are gradually moving back into the area. **http://www.epa.gov/ superfund/kids/site_stories/lovcanal/page_02.htm**

Exhibit 9.2 *The Love Canal Debate (continued)*

Quest(ions) and the Task

It has been at least 40 years since wastes have been dumped at Love Canal. With all of the cleanup efforts that have taken place over the past 25 years, do you think Love Canal would be a good place to live today? Imagine that the following scenario exists: You have been offered a job making $100,000 per year in this particular community. In addition, the housing market is very inexpensive here.

Your task is to analyze the living conditions that exist today in Love Canal. **The essential question you should consider is, *"Is it worth potentially risking our health to obtain material success?"*** Choose a role from the following list and use the goal statements to help you decide. After each team member has made a selection, click on the appropriate role to gain a clear understanding of the issues involved. Would you accept the job and move your family to Love Canal?

Role Goals

Occidental Petroleum Representative **http://www.spa3.k12.sc.us/WebQuests/LoveCanal/ OccidentalPetroleumRepresentative.html**	To eliminate company's liability from dumping of hazardous wastes in Love Canal, NY (says site is safe for residency).
Mayor of Greater Niagara Falls, NY **http://www.spa3.k12.sc.us/WebQuests/LoveCanal/ Mayor.html**	To promote economic growth and tourism of Greater Niagara Falls (Love Canal), NY.
Citizen One **http://www.spa3.k12.sc.us/WebQuests/LoveCanal/ CitizenOne.html**	To encourage residency in Love Canal, NY.
Citizen Two **http://www.spa3.k12.sc.us/WebQuests/LoveCanal/ CitizenTwo.html**	To discourage residency in Love Canal, NY.
Environmentalist **http://www.spa3.k12.sc.us/WebQuests/LoveCanal/ Environmentalist.html**	To protect our earth's natural resources and ensure the safety of habitation in Love Canal (says site is unsafe for residency).

Exhibit 9.2 *The Love Canal Debate (continued)*

Role 1—Occidental Petroleum Representative

Your role as the representative from Occidental Petroleum is going to be to prove to the reader that the Love Canal area is clean and safe to move back into. In August 1978, the Love Canal Interagency Task Force was established to coordinate the many activities undertaken at the canal. The cleanup plan consisted of a tile drain collection system designed to "contain" the wastes and prevent any outward migration of chemical leachate.

A graded trench system was dug around the canal to intercept migrating leachate and create a barrier drain system. The leachate collected from the drain system was pumped to an on-site treatment plant that uses a series of filters, most important, activated charcoal, to remove chemicals from the waste stream. The remaining "clean" water is then flushed down the sanitary sewer system. In June 1994, Occidental Petroleum paid $98 million to cover New York State's cleanup costs, and in December of 1995, Occidental Petroleum paid $129 million to cover the federal government's cleanup costs. In January of 1996, Occidental Chemical (a subsidiary) took over full operation and maintenance of the chemical waste treatment plant at Love Canal.

To find more information about the topic go to **http://www. essential.org/**. While you are researching this site, find support for your role as the Representative of the Occidental Petroleum plant. Find out as many different groups that helped with cleanup as possible. What was done to clean up the site? How much did the cleanup cost? To find more helpful facts visit **http://www.epa.gov/superfund/kids/site_stories/ lovcanal/page_04.htm**.

After you have done your research, you must be able to answer the following questions:

- When did cleanup at Love Canal begin?
- What was done to clean up Love Canal?
- What groups helped clean up Love Canal?
- Why is it safe to live in Love Canal now?

Role 2—Mayor of Greater Niagara Falls (Love Canal), NY

Your role as Mayor is to promote economic growth and tourism in Greater Niagara Falls (Love Canal), New York. You will be able to accomplish this task by attracting new businesses to the community. Business leaders should be given reasons why Greater Niagara Falls

Exhibit 9.2 *The Love Canal Debate* (continued)

(Love Canal) would be a good place for their employees and families to live. While promoting Greater Niagara Falls to a new business, you must discuss (as Mayor) major tourist attractions and recreational/sports activities as well as educational and cultural opportunities.

When preparing your essay, include concerns raised by business leaders with regard to safe living conditions in the Love Canal area. Click on the following sites to research articles with your role and task in mind.

http://buffalocvb.org/Regional_Attractions_0.html
http://www.buffalocvb.org/
http://buffalocvb.org/Sports_and_Recreation_0.html
http://es.epa.gov/oeca/spfund/lovecanl.pdf

Questions
Why do people want to live in Niagara Falls, New York?

What kinds of cultural and recreational activities are available to attract new businesses to the Greater Niagara Falls community?

How much will I save by buying a home in the Love Canal neighborhood?

What was done to clean up the Love Canal neighborhood?

How many families have moved into the Love Canal area since the cleanup began?

Role 3—Citizen One
You are a new citizen in the Love Canal area. You have kept up with the events of Love Canal and are familiar with the cleanup efforts by the Superfund organization. You have been very impressed by these efforts and by the low housing costs in this area. As a matter of fact, people have been moving back into the area so quickly that you were actually placed on a waiting list to move in.

Click here to read how one citizen feels about his new home in Love Canal. Citizen Reaction: **http://www.spa3.k12.sc.us/WebQuests/LoveCanal/citizen.htm**

Exhibit 9.2 *The Love Canal Debate* (continued)

Read this study to find some surprising results regarding health conditions of residents in Love Canal: **http://www.spa3.k12.sc.us/WebQuests/LoveCanal/CanalStudy.htm.**

Questions
Do you consider this a safe community?

Do you consider this a friendly community?

How does the cost of living here compare to other communities?

Role 4—Citizen Two
You are a citizen in the Love Canal area. You have been worried about the reports you have heard about the dangers of nuclear waste. You know that some effort has been made to clean up the dangerous material, but you don't believe it. You are sure that Love Canal is not a safe place to live.

Click on the following sites to read about the concerns of citizens in Love Canal:

http://www.epa.gov/r02earth/superfnd/site_sum/0201290c.htm
http://es.epa.gov/oeca/spfund/lovecanl.pdf
http://Web.globalserve.net/~spinc/atomcc/today.htm

Questions
What evidence can you find that Love Canal is not a safe place to live?

Name two toxic substances that have caused health problems for citizens of Love Canal.

What is one reason Love Canal will never be completely safe?

Role 5—Environmentalist
As an environmentalist, you are concerned about the well-being of our natural resources. You also work to protect people who might be affected by the environment. With respect to Love Canal, you have the primary objectives: (1) to convince current residents of the dangers of continuing to live in Love Canal, and (2) to convince others not to consider moving to Love Canal. Your task is to persuade others that your evidence of the dangers of living in Love Canal is valid.

Exhibit 9.2 *The Love Canal Debate* (continued)

Read excerpts from "The Twentieth Anniversary of Love Canal" at **http://www.spa3.k12.sc.us/WebQuests/LoveCanal/20th Anniversary.html**.

In addition, click on the following sites to view information on the dangers of living in Love Canal:

Medical Study
http://www.spa3.k12.sc.us/WebQuests/LoveCanal/MedicalStudy.htm

Hazardous Wastes
http://www.spa3.k12.sc.us/WebQuests/LoveCanal/definition.htm.
http://Web.globalserve.net/~spinc/atomcc/today.htm

Questions
What are some possible side effects of hazardous waste contamination?

What were some of the problems early residents of Love Canal experienced?

What were the conclusions of the Paigen Study?

Individual Evaluation
Using the information that you have gathered, write a persuasive essay that will convince the reader that Love Canal is a safe place to live today. Be sure to include the following:

- A good topic sentence
- At least three logical reasons supporting your opinion
- A concluding sentence that states how you want the reader to feel
- Proper punctuation, capitalization, and spelling
- Complete sentences
- Organized thoughts

Your completed essay will be evaluated using a rubric.

See **http://www.spa3.k12.sc.us/WebQuests/LoveCanal/ EvaluationRubric.html.**

Exhibit 9.2 *The Love Canal Debate* (continued)

Process

Now that each member of your team has become an expert from one perspective, we're ready to combine what you have learned into a group report. This is not easy because you and your teammates each feel you've found the best solution based upon what is most important to you. However, problems come up. For example, what's good for Occidental Petroleum may not be good for the Environmentalist, and so on. What will you do? In the following group activity, you and your teammates will work through a process to help develop a common **Group Report**.

Create a Group Report at **http://www.spa3.k12.sc.us/WebQuests/ LoveCanal/Debate.html**. (Click on the link to go to the activity.) Prepare to present your findings to the class. All members of the team must contribute to the class presentation.

Resources

Encarta '98: (Articles) "Hazardous Wastes," "Love Canal," and "The Superfund."

Any URL links provided in this WebQuest

Microsoft Word

Video camera

Spartanburg Herald Journal (February 3, 1999) "Contamination 'Hottest I've Ever Seen'" by Matthew K. Pruitt

Evaluation

All members of the team will be assessed for their research and investigation into their chosen roles.

Go to **http://www.spa3.k12.sc.us/WebQuests/LoveCanal/ EvaluationRubric.html** to review the criteria on which your "individual" grades will be based.

In addition, your team will receive a "collaborative grade" for the **group portion** of this project based on the oral presentation.

Exhibit 9.2 *The Love Canal Debate* (continued)

Go to **http://www.spa3.k12.sc.us/WebQuests/LoveCanal/ GroupReportRubric.html** to review the criteria that will determine your "collaborative" grade.

Conclusion

Now that you have completed your research on Love Canal, apply what you have learned to a local situation, The Cowpens, S.C. Brownfield Project. (You can read about this project in the Spartanburg *Herald Journal* listed in the resources.)

The question is, *"Do you think that the old Cowpens Health-Tex site and land around this site is clean and safe?"*

Formulate your conclusions by answering the following questions on paper.

Apply your role from the Love Canal research to the Health-Tex situation. Describe your role.

Will your role take a different outlook in the new situation?

What new questions did this situation bring up?

Did you come up with your own opinion or just go along with your group?

In conclusion, write a paragraph about your feelings regarding the Health-Tex situation and how you think the site should be used.

<u>**Home Connection:**</u> Discuss the Health-Tex situation with your family and find out how they feel about it.

Commentary: This WebQuest does a good job of bringing the issue home for students. The Health-Tex site is literally within walking distance of a local elementary school. This was a topic that teachers had already been discussing with their students in class. Ironically, the teachers who created this activity spent more than three weeks researching ideas before settling on this topic. Even though this was a hot topic right in their own backyard, the Love Canal group spent a great deal of time on the Internet researching other topics and exploring other possibilities. Ultimately, when they decided to pursue developing an activity on this topic, it seemed like the clouds had lifted, and they were able to begin work with a clear vision in mind.

The way that the roles are presented in this WebQuest differ somewhat from other traditional WebQuests. In the "Role Goals" section, the teachers clearly define the position that each role is to take. There is really no ambiguity about what each role is supposed to accomplish, and the information provided leads the students to these conclusions. If this WebQuest were modified, the roles could be defined without explicitly telling the students exactly how their particular role should act or behave.

Exhibit 9.3 *The Northern Spotted Owl Debate*

The Northern Spotted Owl Debate

by Brenda Coleman and Donna Van Vleet

http://www.spa3.k12.sc.us/WebQuests/endangeredanimals/endangered.htm

Overview

This WebQuest is about a situation involving the Northern Spotted Owl and the decline of its natural habitat due to the harvest of timber in the old-growth forest. This activity focuses on a fourth-grade life science unit on Organisms and Their Environment.

Introduction

The Northern Spotted Owl has been the focus of recent controversy because of its special breeding requirements. It does not normally breed in forest areas that have been cut and cleared of trees. In order to breed and raise its young, the spotted owl needs 100 acres of old-growth forest among the redwood, Douglas fir, spruce, and hemlock trees. Spotted owl populations have declined because large areas of forests have been cleared.

In 1990, the United States Fish and Wildlife Service listed the Northern Spotted Owl as a threatened species and limited the legal sale of timber from the areas where the owls usually make their nests. Because the trees in this area are worth $1 million, this has created conflict between the timber industry representatives who want to harvest the valuable timber and protect jobs and conservationists who want to protect old-growth forests.

Exhibit 9.3 *The Northern Spotted Owl Debate (continued)*

The essential question is: *What do we value? Is the price of progress worth the cost to the environment?*

Quest(ions) and the Task

What should the policy be regarding the habitat of the Northern Spotted Owl?

Your task is to research the plight of the timber industry and the Northern Spotted Owl and develop a policy for this issue.

Each team member should choose a role from the following list to gain a clear understanding of the different issues and agencies that are involved in the task.

Roles

Environmentalist

http://www.spa3.k12.sc.us/WebQuests/endangeredanimals/ Role1.htm#environmentilist

Timber Industry Representative

http://www.spa3.k12.sc.us/WebQuests/endangeredanimals/Role2.htm #TimberIndustryRepresentative

Senator from Oregon

http://www.spa3.k12.sc.us/WebQuests/endangeredanimals/Role3.htm #Senator

Business Investor

http://www.spa3.k12.sc.us/WebQuests/endangeredanimals/Role4.htm

Role 1—Environmentalist

An environmentalist is concerned with protecting the environment. You probably want to get an overall view of the relationship between the Northern Spotted Owl and the old-growth forests that provide homes to many animals. Analyze whether or not you think it is important to persuade people to conserve and restore the old-growth forests. Examine the facts to see if there is a need to strive to protect and save the habitats of the Northern Spotted Owl.

View the following site to see information about the old-growth forests:

Exhibit 9.3 *The Northern Spotted Owl Debate* (continued)

http://www.northcoast.com/~elsbree/nspowl.html

View these sites to read about the Northern Spotted Owl:

http://www.owlpages.com/
http://dmoz.org/Society/Issues/Environment/Conservation_and_
    Endangered_Species/
http://www.nwf.org/nwf/kids/cool/leopard1.html

Questions:
Why are the old-growth forests valuable to Oregon?

What is the relationship of the Northern Spotted Owl and other forest
animals to the old-growth forests?

How does population growth in Oregon change the forest environment?
In what ways can we help the wildlife?

What can we do to protect ecosystems?

Role—Timber Industry Representative
Your goal is to preserve the timber industry. Since the forests provide
your livelihood, you need access to timber. How should the policy be
written regarding land use?

View the following sites to find out more about the timber industry:

Social Impact of Northern Spotted Owl
http://www.sweet-home.or.us/forest/owl/index.html

Background Site http://www.forestryinfo.com

http://www.sheridansun.com/news/2000/0809/editorials/09.html

Exhibit 9.3 *The Northern Spotted Owl Debate* (*continued*)

Questions
How many people in Oregon have lost their jobs due to the lack of forests to harvest timber?

Is the timber industry profitable in Oregon at this time?

Does the timber industry have a future in Oregon today?

Role 3—Senator from Oregon
Since you are naturally concerned about keeping a balance between the environmentalists and the timber industry, you may want to compare and contrast the laws regarding restrictions on logging in the old-growth forests. Formulating new laws about the environment and the timber industries may interest you.

View the following sites for information:
http://www.sweet-home.or.us/forest/owl/index.html#Conservation
http://www.forestryinfo.com/
http://contaminants.fws.gov/Issues/Restoration.cfm
http://endangered.fws.gov/esa.html

Questions
What are the federal government restrictions on logging around known owl nests?

What are some possible concerns about protecting the ecosystem in Oregon?

Role 4—Business Investor
You are trying to promote economic growth. Consider tourist attractions such as the forest and its inhabitants. Predict the best way to achieve economic growth.

View the following site for environmental guidelines:
Impacts in Oregon **http://www.forestryinfo.com**

View the following site for a look at timber profits/losses and products:
http://www.sweet-home.or.us/forest/owl/02_WillMills.html

Exhibit 9.3 | *The Northern Spotted Owl Debate* *(continued)*

Questions

What can you do to make the most from timberland while protecting your initial capital investment?

How much should you be willing to do to protect the habitats of the Northern Spotted Owls?

Group Process

Begin investigating the role that you were assigned.

Visit the Web resources for your role.

Using the Web resources, answer the questions assigned to your role.

Present your information in the form of a chart, poster, report, or any creative style that will interest your classmates.

After all of the roles are discussed, the class will brainstorm solutions and reach a consensus regarding the fate of the Northern Spotted Owl.

A class-generated policy will be written to propose ways to manage timber harvesting in Oregon.

Develop your project further through a class discussion evolving around the following questions:

Is the price of progress worth the cost to the environment? Do we value the environment in the American society?

Formulate a final group report assessing the class's overall values regarding the conservation of the environment and the protection of endangered species.

Exhibit 9.3 *The Northern Spotted Owl Debate (continued)*

Evaluation

	Minimum Effort	**Satisfactory**	**Above Average**
Individual Role	Very short answers	Complete answers with details	Well-thought-out answers with supportive evidence
Group Project	Little input into project	Participates in project with ideas and sugestions	Creative presentation of a project that combines individual roles into one whole
Final Report	Reflects only one or two viewpoints	Summarizes the overall feelings of the group	Shows a consensus that is workable in real life

Conclusion

Write a paragraph and/or a poem about your feelings regarding ways that you can help to conserve the earth's resources. For example, one way to help animals would be to support local nature centers or zoos through volunteering time and money. Another example would be to participate in recycling aluminum cans and newspapers. Continue to explore ways to protect your environment. Your actions will reflect your values.

Visit **http://www.nwf.org/nwf/kids/cool/leopard1.html.**

Also, view this site to see a sample poem:
http://www.ga.k12.pa.us/academics/LS/5th/forestpo/fpoemm/ slhforpo.html.

Commentary: A team of two elementary school teachers developed this WebQuest on the habitat destruction of the Northern Spotted Owl to foster awareness on Earth Day. Neither one had ever done a formal activity on this topic. This example is noteworthy for a few reasons. These novice computer users worked in different schools about 15 miles apart. There was virtually no time outside of the three hours that we met each week for them to plan and develop their activity. We all know what is said about necessity. Well, the two worked out a system in which they would share files over the computer network so they could each see what the other was doing. Also, they used e-mail extensively to communicate ideas and revisions during the days between classes.

Exhibit 9.4 *For Love of the Game*

For Love of the Game

First Place Prize in the Ed Oasis MasterSearch Contest, Spring 2000
**http://www.classroom.com/edsoasis/TGuild/Lessons/
forloveofthegame.htm**

http://www.spa3.k12.sc.us/WebQuests/Basketball/index.htm

Notes to Instructor for using this WebQuest and facilitating mock arbitration:
http://www.spa3.k12.sc.us/WebQuests/Basketball/teachernotes.htm

Overview

With the huge salaries earned by some professional basketball players, one questions whether the players are "worth" what they are paid. The essential question explored in this WebQuest is, "What do we value in American society?" The controversy surrounding professional athletes' salaries is complex and multi-faceted. This activity will help students learn how American labor markets operate and how salaries paid to professional athletes influence our values concerning money. This WebQuest is designed for middle school students and focuses on the following content areas:

Mathematics: **http://www.spa3.k12.sc.us/WebQuests/Basketball/Math**
Science: **http://www.spa3.k12.sc.us/WebQuests/Basketball/Science**
Language arts: **http://www.spa3.k12.sc.us/WebQuests/Basketball/**
    Language

Introduction

In 1998, the National Basketball Players Association threatened to strike if the terms of players' new contracts could not be re-negotiated. Many players believed that although they earned relatively high salaries, the NBA was paying them unfairly. For several months negotiations took place between the players and the NBA commissioner, but no agreement could be reached. Ultimately, the NBA commissioner decided to "lock out" the players until a compromise could be reached. For many of the top-paid players, this was an inconvenience, but for a majority of players, the lockout threatened their livelihood. The NBA also had much to lose. Hundreds of millions of dollars in revenues were being lost during the

Exhibit 9.4 *For Love of the Game* (continued)

lockout. Even worse, the NBA commissioner feared that a delayed or cancelled basketball season would cause fans to lose interest in the game and to resent players for appearing to be greedy.

Question/Task

The NBA Players Association is threatening to go on strike again. They don't believe that they are enjoying the full benefits of revenues grossed by the NBA. Each of you will be assigned a role that examines a certain aspect of the professional basketball players' salary controversy.

Specifically, your question is: *"How should players' salaries be structured?"*

After reading information from various sources and answering questions dealing specifically with your role, you will hold a salary arbitration meeting to decide how to structure players' salaries.

Keep in mind the following questions as you research your role and prepare to negotiate.

Why do professional basketball players earn such disproportionately large salaries in relation to other professional athletes in sports such as hockey?

Why are owners and fans willing to foot the bill on these salaries?

Do players deserve such large salaries?

What impact does professional basketball have on the U.S. and global economies?

Do players deserve more than they currently make?

This task will help you better understand how and why people in every profession earn the salaries they do. As you look at the big picture, this task will help you explain and describe your personal values as well as recognize what other Americans value.

Exhibit 9.4 *For Love of the Game* (continued)

Roles

Before investigating your role, be aware that various members of the news press have expressed their views on players' salaries.

Here are some of the reports to help give you some background on the various viewpoints:

Professional athletes deserve high salaries
http://collegian.ksu.edu/issues/v101/su/n166/sports/sports-salaries-sam.html

Argument against players' earning high salaries
http://www.reporternews.com/sports/candy1019.html

Argument for high players' salaries
http://www.sonic.net/elmolino/paper/dec1898/salaries.shtml

Columnist opposes NBA salaries
http://www.alligator.org/edit/issues/96-sumr/960723/c01col.htm

Complete information about the salary cap
http://www.members.home.net/lmcoon/salarycap.htm

NBA lockout facts
http://www.oregonlive.com/todaysnews/9806/st063015.html

Roles
NBA Player (Represents the NBA Players Association)
http://www.spa3.k12.sc.us/WebQuests/Basketball/player.htm

NBA Team Owner
http://www.spa3.k12.sc.us/WebQuests/Basketball/owner.htm

Sports Agent
http://www.spa3.k12.sc.us/WebQuests/Basketball/agent.htm

Professor of Economics
http://www.spa3.k12.sc.us/WebQuests/Basketball/Economist.htm

Legal Scholar of Ethics
http://www.spa3.k12.sc.us/WebQuests/Basketball/LegalScholar.htm

Exhibit 9.4 *For Love of the Game* (*continued*)

Role 1—Professional Basketball Player

We are glad you could take time out of your busy training schedule to attend this salary arbitration meeting. In order to be prepared to present your recommendation for how players' salaries should be structured, there is some important information you need to know.

These questions will help you develop an understanding of the costs and risks professional basketball players face. By carefully analyzing the information, you will be able to write a proposal stating how you want salaries to be structured and why.

Hyperlinks are provided to help you answer the question(s).

What is the real and personal tax rate in South Carolina?

Based on the cost of an 1,800-square-foot-home, what would a 4,000-square-foot home cost?

http://tcrcc.com/cost.htm – Cost of living in South Carolina with other comparisons.

http://www.datamasters.com/cgi-bin/col.pl – Cost of relocation from one state/city to another state/city based on salary.

http://www2.hpe.com/hpedc/cost.html – Cost of living for High Point, NC w/ comparisons to other North Carolina cities.

http://www.infoplease.com/ipa/A0763363.html – Study of national housing costs.

What aspects of your earnings are insurable (e.g., endorsements, contracts)? Do you have to pay after term insurance ends?

Is there an affordable health care plan after you retire? Why or why not?

http://www.jgstarlink.com/wealthcare/profath.htm – Page about insurance for professional athletes.

http://www.aha-ins.com/college_pro_draft.htm – Professional athlete's career-ending disability

http://www.stonehopper.com/atw/pp/pro.html – Cost of injury for professional athletes

Exhibit 9.4 *For Love of the Game* (*continued*)

Where does money go, if it doesn't go to the player?

How do corporations benefit owners?

How does your play affect the economy?

Where does money from TV revenues come from?

How much money is involved with TV?

http://www.members.home.net/lmcoon/salarycap.htm – Complete information about the salary cap

Does racial discrimination affect salaries?

http://news-info.wustl.edu/feature/1997/Oct97-NBAsalary.html – Discusses racial discrimination between black and white players.

What factors affect your salary?

What do the players want from the lockout?

http://www.oregonlive.com/todaysnews/9806/st063015.html – NBA lockout facts

Is there a retirement plan?

What do most players get paid a year?

What kind of TV contract does the NFL have?

Does a superstar make that much of a difference to a team?

What are the salary restrictions and what exceptions are there?

What is the "Basketball Related Income"?

Is there a limit to the length of a contract or raise that a player can receive?

How does age affect the contract?

Are contracts guaranteed?

Exhibit 9.4 *For Love of the Game* (continued)

http://www.members.home.net/lmcoon/salarycap.htm – Complete information about the salary cap

Now that you have a strong understanding of your position, please write a persuasive essay that explains how much players should earn and why, explain the risks and costs you face as a player. Consider what your performance means to professional basketball. What do you think you are worth? By answering these questions, you will then have a proposal to present to the arbitration committee.

Evaluation – **http://www.spa3.k12.sc.us/WebQuests/Basketball/Evaluation**

Return to the Group Process –
http://www.spa3.k12.sc.us/WebQuests/Basketball/Process

Role 2—Owner
We are glad you could take time out of your busy schedule to attend this salary arbitration meeting. In order to be prepared to present your recommendation for how players' salaries should be structured, there is some important information you need to know.

These questions will help you develop an understanding of the costs and risks that you as an owner face. By carefully analyzing the information, you will be able to write a proposal stating how you want salaries to be structured and why.

Hyperlinks are provided to help you answer the question(s).

Should you be concerned with the fans opinions?

Do fans drive the salaries up?

http://www.oregonlive.com/todaysnews/9806/st063004.html – NBA lockout effect on fans

How have the average salaries changed from 1985-1995?

Why is a lockout probable?

What do you want from the lockout?

Exhibit 9.4 *For Love of the Game* *(continued)*

http://fl.mlive.com/pistons/stories/19981113qanda.html – Question-and-answer with David Stern, NBA commissioner

How many of the 29 teams are unprofitable according to the league?

http://www.oregonlive.com/todaysnews/9806/st063004.html – NBA lockout effect on fans

How does the income tax rate affect you?

How does the cost of living in the Southeast compare to other areas?

What is the cost of constructing the coliseum in Charlotte?

What percentage does the committee propose the Hornets pay for the new arena? How much money is that?

Why is the team against that plan?

Why do you want a new arena in Charlotte?

http://www3.nando.net/newsroom/ap/bkb/1995/nba/cha/feat/archive/ 112995/cha36531.html – Hornets sign six-year deal to play in Charlotte Coliseum.

http://www.buildeval.com/dataindex.html – Cost of building a variety of different structures

What is a salary cap?

What is the "Basketball Related Income"?

What are the advantages or disadvantages to the salary cap?

What is the collective bargaining agreement?

http://www.members.home.net/lmcoon/salarycap.htm – Complete information about the salary cap.

Now that you have a strong understanding of your position, please write a persuasive essay that explains how much players should earn and why and explain the risks and costs you face as an owner. Consider factors

Exhibit 9.4 *For Love of the Game* (*continued*)

such as fan opinion, lost revenue, and creating a winning team. By answering these questions, you will then have a proposal to present to the arbitration committee.

Evaluation – **http://www.spa3.k12.sc.us/WebQuests/Basketball/ Evaluation**

Return to the Group Process – **http://www.spa3.k12.sc.us/WebQuests/ Basketball/Process**

Role 3—Agent
We are glad you could take time out of your busy schedule to attend this salary arbitration meeting. In order to be prepared to present your recommendation for how players' salaries should be structured, there is some important information you need to know.

These questions will help you develop an understanding of the costs and risks associated with being a professional sports agent. By carefully analyzing the information, you will be able to write a proposal stating how you want salaries to be structured and why.

Hyperlinks are provided to help you answer the question(s).

What does a sports agent do?

How many people are in the profession?

What is the average salary?

Why do so many people leave the profession each year?

What is the standard commission?

Are most agents successful? What skills are required to be an agent?

Why is "hitting it big" with one or two player contracts vital to surviving as an agent?

Do agents have the best interest of the player in mind?

Exhibit 9.4 *For Love of the Game* (continued)

http://www.careerexperience.com/ – Excellent information about sports agents and their salaries

http://www.sonic.net/elmolino/paper/dec1898/salaries.shtml – Argument for high players' salaries

Now that you have a strong understanding of your position, please write a persuasive essay that explains how much players should earn and why and explain the risks and costs you face as an agent. Consider factors such as fan opinion, opposition from owners, and your ability to continue your career. By answering these questions, you will then have a proposal to present to the arbitration committee.

Evaluation – **http://www.spa3.k12.sc.us/WebQuests/Basketball/ Evaluation**

Return to the Group Process – **http://www.spa3.k12.sc.us/WebQuests/ Basketball/Process**

Role 4—Professor of Economics

We are glad you could take time out of your busy teaching schedule to attend this salary arbitration meeting. In order to be prepared to present your recommendation for how players' salaries should be structured, there is some important information you need to know.

These questions will help you develop an understanding of the economic and social costs and risks associated with professional basketball players going on strike. By carefully analyzing the information, you will be able to write a proposal stating how you want salaries to be structured and why.

Hyperlinks are provided to help you answer the question(s).

How does supply and demand affect salaries?

What is the reasoning for charging high prices at a game?

Are salaries reflective of the athlete's economic importance to society?

What economic transactions take place during a typical game?

What is the effect of sports on the advertising industry?

Exhibit 9.4 *For Love of the Game* (continued)

How does the lockout affect the arenas? How does it affect the cities?

How does the NBA affect local business?

http://www.oregonlive.com/todaysnews/9806/st063015.html – NBA lockout facts

http://www.oregonlive.com/todaysnews/9806/st063004.html – NBA lockout effect on fans

http://abcnews.go.com/sections/business/DailyNews/ nbastrike981221.html – Effect of lockout on municipalities

http://abcnews.go.com/sections/business/DailyNews/ nbareturn990106.html – Economic Impact of NBA season on local businesss

Now that you have a strong understanding of your position, please write a persuasive essay that explains how much players should earn and why. Explain the risks and costs, if any, facing the economy if professional basketball players decide to go on strike. Consider factors such as fan opinion, the views of both players and owners, and economic theory. By answering these questions, you will then have a proposal to present to the arbitration committee.

Evaluation – **http://www.spa3.k12.sc.us/WebQuests/Basketball/ Evaluation**

Return to the Group Process – **http://www.spa3.k12.sc.us/WebQuests/ Basketball/index.htm#Process**

Role 5—Ethics Legal Scholar
We are glad you could take time out of your busy law practice to attend this salary arbitration meeting. In order to be prepared to present your recommendation for how players' salaries should be structured, there is some important information you need to know.

These questions will help you develop an understanding of the ethical issues being discussed. Specifically, what do many Americans value and what are we willing to pay to have the things we want? By carefully analyzing the information, you will be able to write a proposal stating how you want salaries to be structured and why.

Exhibit 9.4 *For Love of the Game (continued)*

Hyperlinks are provided to help you answer the question(s).

How have salaries affected players' education? Their incentive to play?

If you invested $10 a day for the past two millennia, how long would that money pay a professional basketball player?

Compare the athlete's importance to that of the president's.

Are salaries determined by an individual's usefulness to society?

Is it fair for athletes to earn millions of dollars for playing a sport when thousands of people go homeless and without food in our country?

http://www.alligator.org/edit/issues/96-sumr/960723/c01col.htm – Columnist opposes NBA salaries

http://nationalcounseling.com/timeout.html – Crisis in professional sports (violence and high salaries)

Now that you have a strong understanding of your position, please write a persuasive essay that explains how much players should earn and why and explain the ethical issues that should be considered. Consider factors such as what is best for society and whether our society suffers if a relatively small number of individuals make millions of dollars. By answering these questions, you will then have a proposal to present to the arbitration committee.

Evaluation – **http://www.spa3.k12.sc.us/WebQuests/Basketball/ index.htm#Evaluation**

Return to the Group Process – **http://www.spa3.k12.sc.us/WebQuests/ Basketball/index.htm#Process**

Process
Be aware that your role will probably place you in conflict with another person's role. As you are investigating your role, you will be asked questions to help you prepare for the salary arbitration meeting. The questions will ask you to analyze information, provide answers, and write short essays about your role. Finally, you will hold a mock arbitration meeting to negotiate players' salary structure. A neutral third party will conduct

Exhibit 9.4 *For Love of the Game* (continued)

the arbitration meeting. Each member of the arbitration panel will have five minutes, uninterrupted, to argue how the players salaries should be structured. At the end of that time, five minutes will be allowed for any of the other panel members to ask questions or request clarification. Presentations should include a written statement, at least one visual aid, and any other supporting factors such as Web sites, articles, and books. Following this, the arbiter will moderate open debate. The rules and times for the debate will be voted on by the panel members and approved by the arbiter. Keep in mind, your goal is to reach a compromise with all roles involved. You should try to keep in mind the greater good for the group and look outside of your role.

Resolution

Following the debate and after hearing all of the arguments, the individuals representing each role will meet within their own group to develop a proposal that must bring them closer to consensus with the other viewpoints. The proposal can be done using PowerPoint and should outline the major points that the group wants to be part of the final salary structure. After hearing each group's final proposal, the class will vote on which points to adopt. This will be done by a yes/no majority vote. In the event of a tie, the arbiter will cast the deciding vote. Once students have voted on each point, representatives from each group will meet to create a final PowerPoint presentation that outlines the adopted salary structure.

Evaluation

You will be evaluated on the work that you do in this activity. There will be a grade for answering the questions about your role, a grade for the short essay, and a grade for your contribution to the arbitration meeting. Each grade will be subject to specific grading criteria.

Evaluation for Questions
http://www.spa3.k12.sc.us/WebQuests/Basketball/DataCollection.htm

Evaluation for Short Essay
**http://www.spa3.k12.sc.us/WebQuests/Basketball/
PersuasiveRubric.htm**

Contribution and Quality of Presentation at Arbitration Meeting
**http://www.spa3.k12.sc.us/WebQuests/Basketball/
GroupArbitration.htm**

Exhibit 9.4 *For Love of the Game (continued)*

Conclusion

Consider the task you have just completed and think about the following questions. *Use the questions to guide you in writing a short persuasive essay that argues whether or not money is the main factor that determines values in American society.* Your essay will be graded using the Evaluation for Short Essay at **http://www.spa3.k12.sc.us/WebQuests/Basketball/PersuasiveRubric.htm.**

Knowing what you know now, would you have done anything differently? How would you have done it differently? Why?

Was there room for compromise? If so, was arriving at an agreement difficult? Why or why not?

Do you think that you've solved the problem for good, or is the same problem likely to come up again? Why or why not?

Consider the following question: What do you believe are the top five paid jobs/professions in the United States? (This is just a guess, but try to be realistic.) Now, what are the five most important jobs in the United States? Please include this comparison in your essay.

Were you surprised at what you wrote? Were there significant differences between the top five paid jobs and the five most important jobs? Did what you write help you to understand how our values determine salaries? Why or why not?

What would you suggest to improve this project? Could you see other roles becoming involved? What was difficult for you? Were the directions clear?

Was the purpose of the activity explained clearly?

Commentary: This WebQuest, which won best lesson plan honors after being submitted to Ed Oasis <**http://www.classroom.com/edsoasis/TGuild/Lessons/forloveofthegame.htm**>, exhibits all of the qualities of a fully developed WebQuest. From the beginning, the teachers "hook" the students with an interesting introduction. Although students will be learning a variety of math, science, and language arts skills, the vehicle through which the learning will take place is interesting and relevant to them. Recalling the discussion on essential questions *(see Chapter 3)*, it should be noted that the essential question in this activity required a great deal of deliberation and fine-tuning. As with many successful WebQuests, essential questions that probe human values tend to extend students' thinking.

A second notable feature of this WebQuest is the well-thought-out, highly defined roles. Not all topics lend themselves to developing materials from a variety of perspectives on issues that polarize the participants. These teachers do an exceptional job at identifying "real life" participants in this debate. This process also takes significant time and planning because certain roles that may seem promising in the beginning may not be supported by information available on the Internet.

Throughout this WebQuest, students, whether investigating their group roles or participating in a mock arbitration, are constantly being required to build on past knowledge and to connect that knowledge with new ideas to form original thoughts and opinions. Once again, it is readily apparent that good instructional practice is the reason for the success of this activity. Not only good instruction but also teamwork between the teachers and their willingness to support each other—as well accept support from others—makes this an outstanding WebQuest.

Technical Corner

For technical assistance with the topics discussed in this chapter, please refer to the Appendix.

Skill	Description	Appendix Page Number
Chapter 8 Technical Corner		
Using Sound in Web Pages	With multimedia tools becoming more prevalent, adding sound and music to Web pages is a good skill to help jazz up any activity. Discusses acquiring sound files through commercial and no-cost means.	199
Linking to a Sound File	Demonstrates creating hyper-links to sound files.	200
Plug-Ins and Add-Ins	Discusses the usefulness and popularity of special software that both enhances and facili-tates your Internet browsing experience. Several popular plug-ins are described, and URLs are provided.	202

Chapter *10*

What Lies Beyond?

"The mind is not a vessel to be filled, but a flame to be kindled."
— Plutarch

Students must become critical consumers of information. If they can assess various information resources and gain a range of perspectives, they will have a better chance at achieving success in the 21st century. As educators, our job is to show them how to corral that data and put it to good use.

By providing students opportunities to interact with information, teachers are able to enrich the learning experience so that students can become skilled at making wise and informed choices about the vast information that confronts them. At the same time, we must reassure ourselves. Using educational technology for learning and teaching is challenging. It does not come easy.

Information is often transient and sometimes ethereal on the Web. As teachers, we have no control of the Web—except for the information we post ourselves. Textbooks have always been the convenient alternative—static and predictable. The Web is fluid. By emphasizing the skills necessary to evaluate information, students acquire a lifelong learning skill. That is one of the most important legacies that we can give children today.

The more information that students become exposed to the greater the chance that they will become critical consumers of information. Students must be able to determine the veracity of a source and of the information that is presented. What is read is not always what is true. As students learn to evaluate and to synthesize information from a variety of sources, they become better able to interact with the world.

By exposing students to the real-world application of knowledge, we emphasize the importance of learning by doing, creating, and exploring. The cooperative learning strategies that we have emphasized from the beginning of The Web-Based Learning Model provide active learning experiences for all children.

We know that for some students, a virtual "learning eruption" occurs when they are allowed to actively engage in applying what they have learned, as they do when participating in a WebQuest. Some students, on the other hand, require sequential steps that are structured, as are the steps of a Guided Tour or CyberInquiry. We also know that few students learn best when they are exposed to an hour-long lecture. To learn best, students must be actively involved with their learning.

Using the Conceptual Framework

The conceptual model for Web-based learning is not intended to be a sequential model for students. Students do not necessarily move linearly from a Guided Tour to a WebQuest. The process steps outline a method for teachers to become familiar with the Web. As teachers become more comfortable with using technology, they will be more willing to take risks in developing projects. Using the same topic in creating the early models—the Guided Tours and the Scavenger Hunts—provides a teacher with background information and the extensive research that is necessary before beginning a WebQuest.

Students are at different levels of understanding. In the early stages of learning, a child may need the structured experience of a Guided Tour. The model is also useful for a student who may be comfortable with constructing his or her own knowledge but may not have had previous experience using a computer. At the same time, another group of students may be ready to use the Web to research their own information (Internet Discovery). Still another group may be ready to undertake a WebQuest.

All of these activities may be going on in the same classroom, at the same time, if a teacher has multiple computers. We have been in classrooms where the teacher has rotated students through learning stations. In cooperative learning groups, they began work at a developmentally appropriate level. Although each child rotated through each learning station and the teacher had high academic expectations for all students, the student completed work that was appropriate for his or her learning stage.

So it is with the conceptual framework. While the Guided Tour may have extensions that encourage students to transform information, the main purpose is to explore information—generally at an introductory level. The conceptual framework moves up through Bloom's Taxonomy.

We scaffold learning so that it is appropriate for students at their individual levels. Through carefully developing an essential question, the teacher keeps clearly in mind the direction that all students are heading. However, not all students arrive at the destination at the same time.

Some students will not be at the computers. In one class, the teacher had developed several Web-based activities for students. However, the day we were visiting her classroom, she had one group at the computer working on a Guided Tour and other groups at their desks working on a stock market unit. Both activities reinforced what the teacher was teaching at that time.

The Education Dilemma

**The empires of the future
are the empires of the mind.**
— *Sir Winston Churchill*

Contrary to the beliefs of some, technology use in public education is different from technology use in business and industry. We hear the call that technology must prepare students for the "real world." We can only wonder what "real world" that is.

In the real world of today, people use computers to be productive at their job and at home. They write programs, make presentations, formulate budgets, and balance their checkbooks. The programs that are used for these activities today may not be used tomorrow. Public schools are not in the business of training students to be skilled workers for XYZ Company. We are in the business of helping students as they soar—of helping students learn to think independently and confidently.

Teachers help students become better learners, better thinkers, better information consumers, and better problem solvers. Admittedly, some of the skills learned in school will someday be used on the job, but we should not treat schools as training centers for the business sector. Our entire approach to using technology in schools must focus on using computers as a means to increase students' ability to think and use information—rather than as a business tool. Computers are our tools of the trade.

It is quite common to hear that we must prepare students for the 21st century. What we really need to look at closely is what type of preparation is intended. Developing higher-order thinking skills and problem solving abilities are the types of preparation that students should receive from working with technology in schools.

The Value of Technology?

**Spoon feeding in the long run teaches us
nothing but the shape of the spoon."**
— E.M. Forster

One of the quandaries that we have faced is when to begin using technology with students. If our focus is on developmentally appropriate learning activities that foster higher-level thinking skills, the answer is clear. We begin using the technology whenever there are appropriate learning activities. In the hands of a gifted teacher, that beginning may occur very early in a child's career. If, however, the teacher's understanding of technology is intricately woven into software programs that emphasize "electronic worksheets," the computer programs may indeed stifle the natural curiosity and love for learning that young children bring to school.

The teacher determines the usefulness of technology in a classroom. Technology cannot transform a good teacher into a bad one or a bad teacher into a good one. A good teacher uses a variety of methods—developmentally appropriate methods—to spur students to greater heights. Introspective and self-critical, good teachers repeatedly ask themselves, *"How can I improve the lesson? What can I do to make students understand and move forward?"* Good teachers do not accept the status quo.

Teachers who employ the computer as another medium through which instruction takes place, with the end result of fostering higher-order thinking skills, optimize the student's learning. That is true whatever the student's age.

The Next Step

**When you make the finding yourself
—even if you're the last person on Earth to see the light
—you'll never forget it.**
— Carl Sagan

The technology that we use today will continue to become more pervasive and less conspicuous. This will hold true in schools as well. Just as we flip on a light switch without a second thought, teachers will learn to use technology for instruction as if they were using a textbook or blackboard. At some point, teachers will be able to seamlessly incorporate technology into their lessons so that students will not be "sitting in front of the computer," but instead will be engaged in challenging assignments that make use of the available technology. At that point, teachers will have ascended well beyond the conceptual framework of which we write. As with all good teaching skills, they will have the objective clearly in mind and use whatever techniques are necessary to increase student success. They will blend models—using what works best for their children and abandoning the rest.

Professional Development

Toward this goal, school districts must continue their commitment to providing quality technology training to teachers to enable them to make this transition. As we are all aware, teachers consistently call for training on using technology. They desperately want to use technology to assist in their lesson planning and want to make sure they are doing so in an effective manner and in the students' best interest. In part, what has prevented this expansion of the effort is the old "chicken or egg" story. Where does one put the limited funds available? Do we spend funds on technology hardware and ignore the training, or do we provide the training and limit the hardware?

In order to succeed, we must do both. We must be sure an adequate infrastructure is in place, and we must provide high-quality training. The training must focus on integrating the technology into the classroom. The continued focus of training on productivity, on using the software to increase our ability to create tests, or to grade students, or to learn to word process, must shift. Each training course must emphasize how that *productivity* tool can be transformed into a teaching tool.

The One-Computer Classroom

All things begin small. Computers generally arrive in classrooms one by one. School budgets are rarely able to fully implement technology plans. One of the most frequent concerns that we hear voiced by teachers is, "I can't use technology in my classroom because I only have one computer."

As a result, computer labs have become synonymous with using technology to deliver classroom instruction. That is unfortunate. That is one of the reasons that unbridled criticism has come our way. Computer labs tend to emphasize "one size fits all" instruction. If one student would benefit from using an academic remediation/acceleration software package, then all students should benefit. We all know that is not necessarily true.

It really comes down to instructional strategies and changing the way we teach. In a one-computer classroom, the teacher must first decide to use the computer with students. Many teachers have shared with us that if they had multiple computers in their classroom, they would be happy to allow students to work on them. With one computer, however, they were worried the students might damage it or get into their files. These are legitimate concerns, but the concerns do not merit banning students from using the computer. With clear expectations for student behavior and consequences for not meeting these expectations, teachers may put aside that concern.

The steps in the Web-based learning framework are ideal for conducting one-computer instruction. Each of the six process steps is tailored for small groups of students to use. Students share research responsibilities and information. Even for a WebQuest, the one-computer classroom adjusts well.

Ready...Set...

If some or most of the material covered in this book was new to you, it may seem a bit overwhelming. You'll find reassurance in the fact that these activities work and teachers enjoy creating them for their students. It would be one thing to tout yet another educational model that belongs only in a theory textbook; however, we have seen firsthand the tremendous success that both teachers and students achieve when they follow The Web-Based Learning Model. Teachers, even the most hesitant ones, become engrossed in the instructional value of developing these activities.

The model levels the playing field for the teacher who is not a "techno-wiz." Because teachers complete many of the activities using templates, they do not feel the pressure to learn all of the technical skills right away. They have ample time to focus on good instruction. For the technically advanced teacher, these activities provide fertile ground to try out instructional ideas only dreamed of a few years ago.

Ultimately, students are the real winners. The Web-Based Learning Model challenges students in new ways and motivates them to expand their thinking. Teachers who exclusively hold on to teaching methods that were effective 20 years ago should take this unprecedented opportunity to shape instructional delivery that will prepare students during the new century. It will take effort, and it will take change, but we feel assured that teachers who are exceptional in every sense of the word will adopt this model. In doing so, they will continue to help students unlock the doors to knowledge and build the foundations for their futures.

Ready...Set...GO!

Technology Corner Matrix of Skills

Skill	Description	Appendix Page Number
Chapter 4 Technical Corner		
Copying and Pasting Between Programs	Allows user to copy Web site URL and paste it into a word processor or Web page editor.	181
File and Bookmark Management	Details importance of maintaining organized system of files and Internet sites in creating Web-based learning activities. Demonstrates saving, naming, and creating files and folders.	183
Chapter 5 Technical Corner		
What Is a Web Page?	Discusses importance of Web page as a means of sharing information and conveying clear content. Steps are outlined that demonstrate how to create Web pages from scratch or by using Web page templates.	188
Chapter 6 Technical Corner		
Creating Tables	Explains vital role tables play in creating Web pages and demonstrates how to create and modify tables.	191
Creating Links to Web Sites Using Text in MS Word 2000	Hyperlinks are the glue that connects Web pages to one another. This section demonstrates how to create hyperlinks to outside URLs.	192
Linking Pages in Your Web Project Using MS Word 2000	Linking together Web pages in a project is an important skill. Learn how to connect a multi-page Internet activity.	194
Posting Web Pages to a Web Site	Basic steps and resources are explained that will allow you and your students to publish your work on the World Wide Web.	195

Skill	Description	Appendix Page Number
Chapter 8 Technical Corner		
Multi-Tasking	Multi-tasking involves simultaneously running multiple software programs and switching between them to perform a variety of functions. This skill is essential when developing Web-based learning activities.	197
Chapter 9 Technical Corner		
Using Sound in Web Pages	With multimedia tools becoming more prevalent, adding sound and music to Web pages is a good skill to help jazz up any activity. Discusses acquiring sound files through commercial and no-cost means.	199
Linking to a Sound File	Demonstrates creating hyperlinks to sound files.	200
Plug-Ins and Add-Ins	Discusses the usefulness and popularity of special software that both enhances and facilitates your Internet browsing experience. Several popular plug-ins are described, and URLs are provided.	202

Chapter 4 Technical Corner

The Technical Corner emphasizes those technical skills necessary to complete the activities in each chapter. The prerequisite skills required would be keyboarding and opening and closing an Internet browser and a word processing program. In the interest of brevity, we have focused on the Microsoft Office Suite of programs in this book.

The following directions explain how to copy an Internet address (URL) and paste that URL into another file, such as a word processing document or Web page. These skills will become essential in developing each activity within the framework.

Copying and Pasting Between Programs

Students should open their Internet browser first and then open the word processor program. At the bottom of the screen, two icons will appear that represent each open program. Students should be made aware that clicking on either of the icons will switch them between the Internet browser and the word processing program. In this example, we use Microsoft Word as the word processing program. Ask the students to copy a Web site address from the Internet browser to the word processor using the following steps:

1. When the Internet browser first launches, a preset Web site will load. This Web site was probably set to load automatically by a lab manager or by the person who uses that computer. Therefore, the site that loads may not necessarily be useful for a specific activity.

2. If the Web site that loads does not appear to be useful for the activity, it is often helpful to designate a particular Web site as a starting point.

3. In classes that we teach, we ask teachers to navigate to the Spartanburg (South Carolina) School District 3 Web site. They do this by clicking in the address box near the top of the Internet browser window, typing in the address (URL) **<http://www.spa3.k12.sc.us>**, and then pressing the "Enter" key on the keyboard.

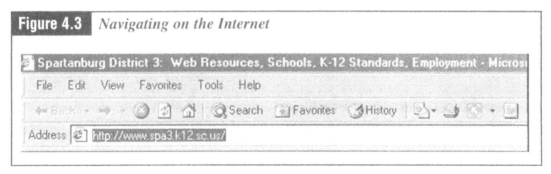

Figure 4.3 *Navigating on the Internet*

Microsoft® Internet Explorer 5.0 screen shot reprinted by permission from Microsoft Corporation.

4. This will access the Spartanburg School District 3 Web site. Once on the Web site, *we ask teachers to click on the hyperlink near the top of the page that says: "Search over 72 popular search engines and the Spartanburg District 3 Web site!"* A hyperlink is usually text, which is underlined, or a graphic that allows the user to click and be transported to another page in the Web site or a different Web site altogether. When placed over a hyperlink, the mouse arrow may turn into a little pointing hand.

5. Clicking on this hyperlink will open a page that contains links to dozens of search engines. *(Chapter 5 discusses in detail how to use search engines.)*

6. We then discuss with the class the advantages and disadvantages of using one search engine over another. Typically, a search engine is a good place to start developing each activity in the framework. Once Web sites have been located using search engines, teachers may follow hyperlinks and begin to explore other Web sites.

7. Once a search engine has been used to generate lists of useful Web sites, it is time to begin copying the Web addresses (URLs) from the Internet browser and pasting the URLs into a word processor.

8. In computer language, "copying" refers to clicking and dragging the mouse pointer over some text (such as a URL), highlighting the text, and then copying the text to the computer's memory. "Pasting" would then be telling the computer where to insert the text that has been copied.

9. With the Internet browser open, click and drag the mouse over the Web site address (URL) in the address box located at the top of the browser program to highlight the URL.

10. Locate the "Edit" menu and click on it one time. Locate the menu option that says "Copy" and click on it one time. The URL has now been temporarily copied to the computer's memory. The reason that this is temporary is that if the computer were turned off or if it lost power, the material that was copied would be lost. Also, only newer software will allow the user to copy more than one item at a time. Therefore, each time a new item is copied, the previous item copied is wiped out of the computer's memory.

11. Click on the application icon at the bottom of the screen that will be used to edit the activity (in this example, MS Word). The program will become active, and the contents of the Internet browser will no longer be visible.

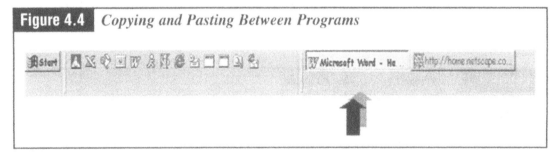

Figure 4.4 *Copying and Pasting Between Programs*

Microsoft® Windows 2000 screen shot reprinted by permission from Microsoft Corporation.

12. Click to place the cursor in the desired location on the page. Generally speaking, place the cursor toward the left margin of the word processing document. Locate and click on the "Edit" menu and then locate and click on the" Paste" menu item. The URL that was selected and copied will now be pasted into the Word document.

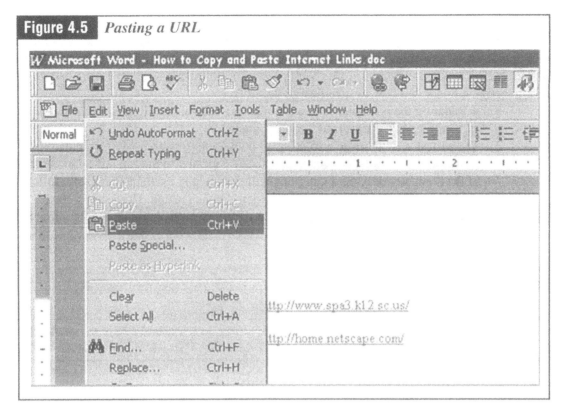

Figure 4.5 *Pasting a URL*

Microsoft® Word 2000 screen shot reprinted by permission from Microsoft Corporation.

13. To gather more addresses from the Internet browser, return to the browser by clicking on the icon at the bottom of the screen.
14. Repeat steps 9-12.

Copying and pasting are two of the most valuable technical skills that a teacher can develop. Not only does copying and pasting allow for accuracy when saving URLs to a file but these skills also are transferable through virtually every Windows-based computer program. For example, if a teacher has two different tests on the word processor and wants to combine certain questions from each test, re-typing questions would be a waste of time. Instead, the teacher can simply highlight (by clicking and dragging with the mouse) the questions from one test... click on the "Edit" menu and choose "Copy," then open the other test and choose "Edit," then "Paste." While it's not exactly striking oil, copying and pasting can translate into many hours of saved time.

File and Bookmark Management

Out of all of the topics and software that we teach, nothing receives a bigger, longer, glassier stare than the subject of "file management." Some may think to themselves, *Honestly, do I really need to "manage" my files? They seem to be taking care of themselves quite nicely without my help. What exactly is a file? Are my word processing documents considered files? What about my spreadsheets? Are they files? I've got a picture of my dog saved on the computer; is that a file too?*

YES!! They are ALL files. Computers contain essentially two things: files and folders. Folders hold files. Just like the filing cabinet that contains folders with files inside of them, your computer has many folders that contain files inside of them.

File management keeps us organized. Anyone who has used a computer knows that searching for a "lost" file right before class begins is frustrating. How do we avoid those problems? We learn how to manage our files.

File Management

To be successful in creating Internet activities and Web pages, knowing and understanding how and where to save files is important. Being able to create folders and save files to these folders is critical when we start creating Web pages. The following steps will demonstrate how to create a folder and how to save files to that folder.

1. A folder on the computer is like a folder in a file cabinet. Its purpose is to help us save files in an organized, efficient manner.
2. The easiest way to create a folder is to double-click on the "My Computer" icon in Windows 95/98/2000. This icon is usually located in the top left-hand corner of the computer desktop. Doing this will display any available hard drives, floppy drives, or network drives where folders can be created. Drives are actual physical disks located in a computer or disks placed in a computer that allow for storage of data.

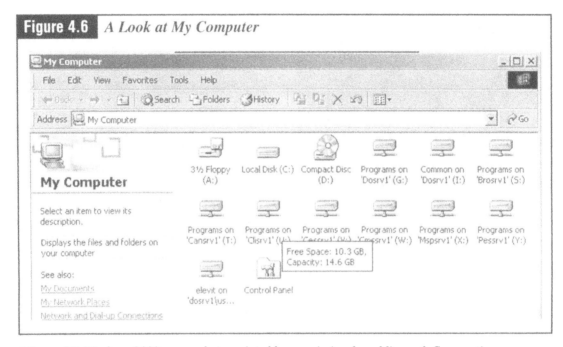

Figure 4.6 *A Look at My Computer*

Microsoft® Windows 2000 screen shot reprinted by permission from Microsoft Corporation.

3. Determining where to create folders is important. Creating a folder on a computer's hard drive is useful if that particular computer is accessible whenever one is working on an activity. The hard drive is physically located in that particular computer. Therefore, without access to that computer, it is not possible to gain access to the files and folders associated with the activity. A floppy disk offers a bit more flexibility because folders and files can be saved to it, and the disk can then be used in any computer that can read that disk. The main constraint is that floppy disks are limited in how much data can be stored on them. A network drive is useful for saving files because it can store large amounts of data and can be accessed from any computer that is connected to the network. However, if the network goes down, or if a computer is not on the network, accessing a network drive is not possible.
4. In this example, create a folder on the C: drive (hard drive) by first double-clicking on the icon for the C: drive.
5. A folder can be created at this point, or double-click on an existing folder to create what is called a *subfolder*.

6. In this example, we will create a folder on the C: drive called "My Project."

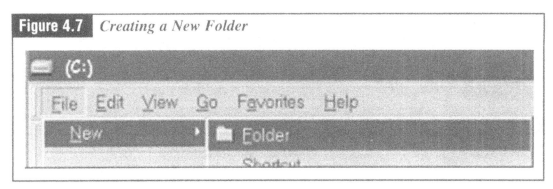

Microsoft® Windows 2000 screen shot reprinted by permission from Microsoft Corporation.

7. Locate and click on the "File" menu and choose "New... Folder."
8. This will place a new folder on your C: drive.
   Click in the highlighted area next to the folder and type in a desired folder name such as "My Project" (without quotation marks).

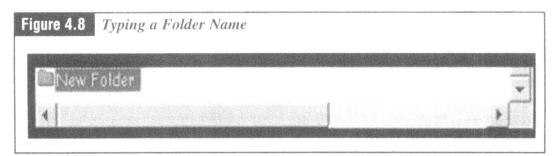

Microsoft® Windows 2000 screen shot reprinted by permission from Microsoft Corporation.

Saving Files to a Folder

After a folder has been created, it is very easy to save files that have been created or downloaded from the Internet.

1. When working in a program such as Word 2000, the first step that should be taken is to save and name the file that is being edited.
2. To save a file, locate the "File" menu and click on it one time. Locate the "Save As" menu option and click one time. This procedure is used in three cases:
   1. When saving a file for the first time.
   2. When saving an existing file to a new location. For example, a file may have been opened from a floppy disk, and the user wants to save a copy of the file to the hard drive on the computer.
   3. When making changes to an existing file and saving the changed file under a different name.

For example, a teacher may be working on a file named "Test I." She alters the test for a different class by removing several of the questions. Because she doesn't want to overwrite her original Test I file, she would choose "File... Save As" and name the file something like "Test II." Now, the teacher would have two separate files, one for each test.

3. After clicking on "File" and "Save As," navigate to the folder that was designated for the activity. Do this by clicking on the drop-down arrow to the right of the "Save In" folder.
4. Once the folder has been located, double-click on the folder to open it.
5. Put the cursor in the File Name box, name the file, and then click Save.

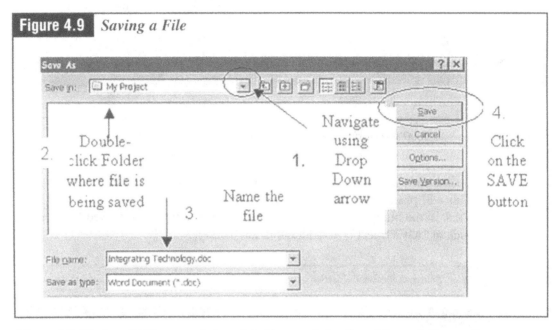

Figure 4.9 *Saving a File*

Microsoft® Windows 2000 screen shot reprinted by permission from Microsoft Corporation.

Bookmarking Web Sites

Bookmarking is the process of marking a Web site in your browser so that it can be visited again (without the user having to remember the address). Teachers find that bookmarking allows them to steer students to particular sites. For example, a teacher may bookmark a series of Web sites in a folder, which features a topic that the students are studying (e.g., volcanoes, earthquakes, cells).

1. To begin, launch the Internet browser. Before attempting to bookmark, the teacher must have some idea of how to get started finding Web sites to bookmark. Recall the discussion at the beginning of this section. It is useful to have a starting point on the Internet when beginning to develop Internet activities. As mentioned, we instruct our teachers to type in the URL for the Spartanburg School District 3 Web site **<http://www.spa3.k12.sc.us>** and then press the "Enter" key on the keyboard. Once they have reached the district Web site, we ask them to click on the hyperlinked text that says, **"Search over 72 popular search engines and the Spartanburg District 3 Web site!"**
2. The teachers will then have a long list of search engines that they can click on to begin the process of locating Web sites. *(Chapter 5 discusses in detail how to effectively use search engines.)* They could then begin following hyperlinks that were generated using the search engines.
3. A teacher may already be familiar with a particular Web site address through advertisements, magazines, or television. If this is the case, the teacher may type in the address of the Web site to pull it up.
4. *(Use caution: Typing Web site addresses not only raises the probability of typographical errors, but, in some cases, may inadvertently load inappropriate Web sites.)* Please see the screen shot (Microsoft Internet Explorer 5.0) in Figure 4.10 to see where to type the URL.

Figure 4.10 *Internet Browser Address Bar*

Microsoft® Internet Explorer 5.0 screen shot reprinted by permission from Microsoft Corporation.

5. For example, after you have typed in the popular search engine address shown in Figure 4.10 and pressed "Enter," the Web site will load. It is possible to add this URL to the "Favorites" folder for future reference.
6. To do so, click on the "Favorites" menu and choose "Add to Favorites" as seen in Figure 4.11. When prompted, click "OK."

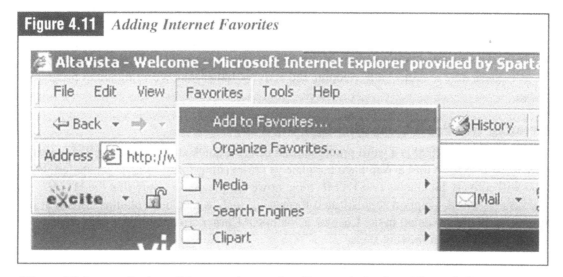

Figure 4.11 *Adding Internet Favorites*

Microsoft® Internet Explorer 5.0 screen shot reprinted by permission from Microsoft Corporation.

To return to that Web site, simply click on the "Favorites menu" and click on the site you wish to visit.

Chapter 5 Technical Corner

In Chapter 4, we demonstrated some of the skills necessary to be successful with The Web-Based Learning Model. We started with some fundamental skills, such as copying and pasting and file management. As teachers become comfortable with the format of these activities, more advanced training leads them to constructing Web pages.

The reason for teaching Web page development is very simple. The Internet provides a forum for teachers to create communities of learners. What is developed for one classroom may be used in hundreds of classrooms. We need to share these Web-based activities. Additionally, students can quickly access activities that are in a Web page format either from an Internet browser or on a local school network.

By creating Guided Tours and Scavenger Hunts as Web pages, teachers can post these activities on a district Web site to be used by any students with Internet access. This section will provide an overview of the basics of creating a Web page. In the Technical Corners of the following chapters, we will discuss more advanced features of Web page design, such as layout, graphics, and hyperlinks.

What Is a Web Page?

A Web page is a file or document that is posted on the Internet, a school network, or even on an individual computer. The primary purpose of a Web page is to convey clear content and information. Web pages contain code called Hypertext Markup Language (HTML). The software demonstrated in this section automatically converts most work into HTML, so there is more time to focus on developing the activity, rather than worrying about programming.

Creating Web Pages Using Microsoft Word 2000

Microsoft® Word 2000 is a word processor that offers a quick start to creating Web pages. MS Word 2000 provides a Web page template (a pre-existing form) to help get started. Word also will convert documents into HTML files; however, please be aware that the HTML conversion will not support sophisticated formatting such as tabs and columns. This will be discussed in greater detail in the Chapter 6 Technical Corner. To create Web pages using Word 2000, do the following steps:

1. Locate and run Word 2000.
2. Click on the "File" menu and choose "New," as shown in Figure 5.4.

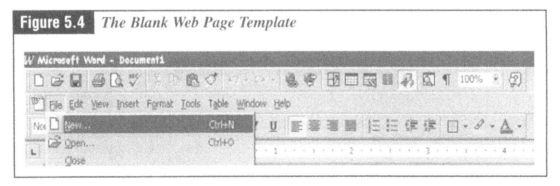

Figure 5.4 *The Blank Web Page Template*

Microsoft® Word 2000 screen shot reprinted by permission from Microsoft Corporation.

1. Click on the "Web Pages" tab, then double-click on "Blank Web Page."

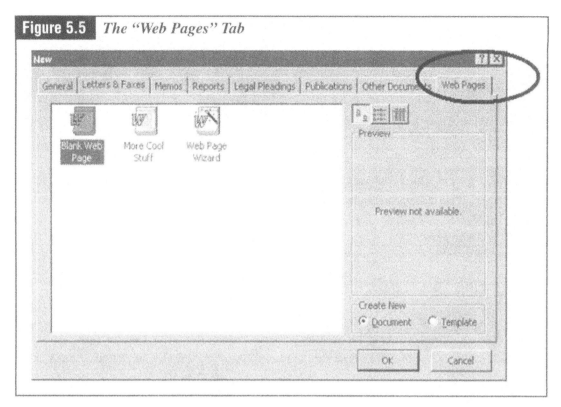

Figure 5.5 *The "Web Pages" Tab*

Microsoft® Word 2000 screen shot reprinted by permission from Microsoft Corporation.

2. A blank Web page will appear.
3. The next step should always be to save the Web page by choosing "File" and "Save As."
4. File names for Web pages should be short, one-word, descriptive names with no spaces. For example, a Web page titled "Ms. Smith's Home Page" could be saved as "smithindex.html" (without the quotation marks).
5. To add the full title for the Web page, choose "File" then "Properties." Type the desired title, click "OK," and that is what will appear in the title bar.

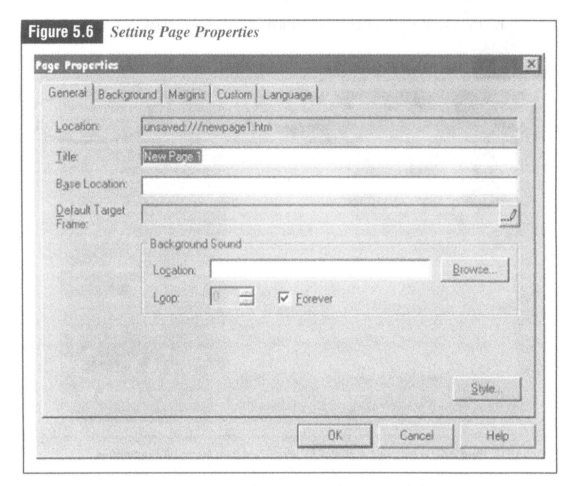

Figure 5.6 *Setting Page Properties*

Microsoft® Word 2000 screen shot reprinted by permission from Microsoft Corporation.

Although it may not seem like it, these steps are all that are required to get a Web page off the ground. Providing content is the next step in making the Web page into something useful. For example, creating a Guided Tour at this point would simply require copying and pasting *(see Chapter 4)* one or many URLs into a blank Web page and then typing the objectives, standards, and questions that go along with the activity. A Scavenger Hunt would require that teacher to copy and paste the URL of a search engine and then type the topic, concept, essential question, objectives, and standards for the activity.

Chapter 6 Technical Corner

In the Chapter 5 Technical Corner, we demonstrated how to create a blank Web page. For the most part, it was not too much different from regular word processing. The purpose of creating a Web page in Chapter 5 was to show how teachers could develop Guided Tours and Scavenger Hunts on Web pages to post on the Internet or on a school district's local network.

In this Technical Corner, we broaden the usefulness of a Web page to serve a variety of purposes. The Web page can be used to help teachers communicate with parents and students, showcase student work, and provide instructional content. Although a teacher's Web page generally focuses on information the teacher wants to convey (class rules, assignments, important dates), it can also be a place where teachers link to instructional activities developed in the Web-based learning framework. This section will highlight some fundamental skills that demonstrate how to align content on a Web page, how to link activities to Web sites, how to link Web pages together, and how to post a Web page on the Internet.

Creating Tables

Learning to create tables is one of the skills most widely used when creating Web pages. Unlike regular word processing documents, a Web page will not take kindly to using the tab key or the space bar to position text. In fact, several programs will not allow users to use the tab key on a Web page and prompts them to insert a table instead. Tables also serve an important function when using text with graphics on a Web page.

A word processor allows the user to click-and-drag clip art anywhere on the page; however, a Web page is not that flexible. Therefore, creating and using tables is the best bet when it comes to trying to get text, pictures, or both aligned correctly on a Web page. At first, one of the things our students have the most trouble doing is placing a picture on a Web page and then typing some text either immediately to the left or to the right of the picture. However, when we demonstrate how to use a table to accomplish this common task, most of the confusion is cleared up. Here is an example:

In this example, it would have been impossible to place the text directly next to the graphic without using a table to align the two items. Use the following simple instructions to create a table.

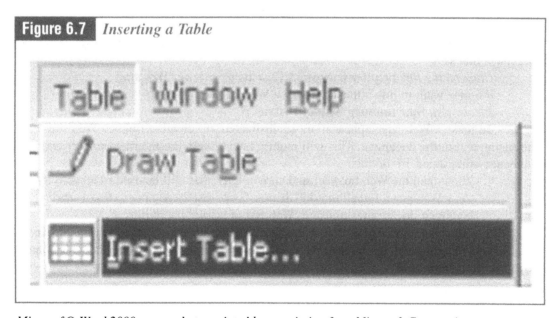

Microsoft® Word 2000 screen shot reprinted by permission from Microsoft Corporation.

1. Open a Word 2000 document.
2. Choose "Table" and then "Insert Table."
3. Decide how many columns and rows to make the table.

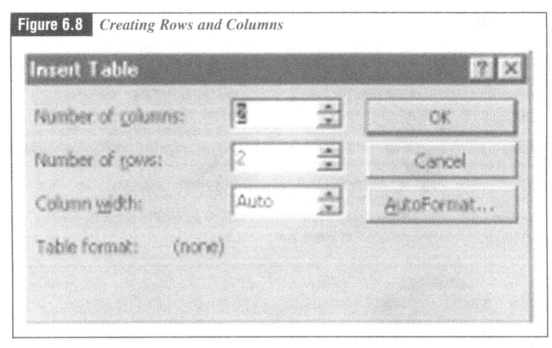

Figure 6.8 *Creating Rows and Columns*

Microsoft® Word 2000 screen shot reprinted by permission from Microsoft Corporation.

4. Click "OK," and the table will be inserted in the document.

Creating Links to Web Sites Using Text in MS Word 2000

In Chapter 4, we explained how to copy and paste the URL from the address bar in a Web browser to a word processor or Web page file. The purpose of this was to create a hotlist of annotated Web sites or to collect Web sites for a Guided Tour. Following this process, one would simply copy a URL (e.g., **http://www.spa3.k12.sc.us**) and paste it into a document.

As we refine our eye for Web page design, there may be times when we want a user to click on a line of text that acts as a hyperlink. For example, instead of creating a line on a Web page that says:

Click on the link **http://www.spa3.k12.sc.us** *to visit our Web site.*

We may want to link a line of text to a Web site like this:

Please visit **Spartanburg School District 3**.

To make a Web page appear more sophisticated, try creating links to Web sites or files using text in the document. This will require having both the Internet browser and a Web page editor open. To do this:

1. First open the Web browser and copy a URL that will be used in an activity or on a Web page. Recall that in Chapter 5, we discussed how to use a search engine to locate sites to use in Web-based learning activities.

2. To create a hyperlink to a Web site using text, first highlight (by clicking-and-dragging with the mouse) the text in the Web page that is intended to become the hyperlink.

| Figure 6.9 | *Creating a Hyperlink* |

Click here to go to Yahoo's search engine.

3. Locate the "Insert" menu and select the "Hyperlink" menu item.
4. Place the mouse cursor in the first empty box (labeled "Link to file or URL:") and click one time in the box.
5. Use the keyboard combination of "Ctrl+V" to paste the URL, then click on "OK." Normally, we could have right-clicked with the mouse and selected "Paste" from the menu, but that feature is not available here. So, we must use the keyboard command by holding down the "Ctrl" button and pressing the "V" button at the same time.

| Figure 6.10 | *The "Insert Hyperlink" Screen* |

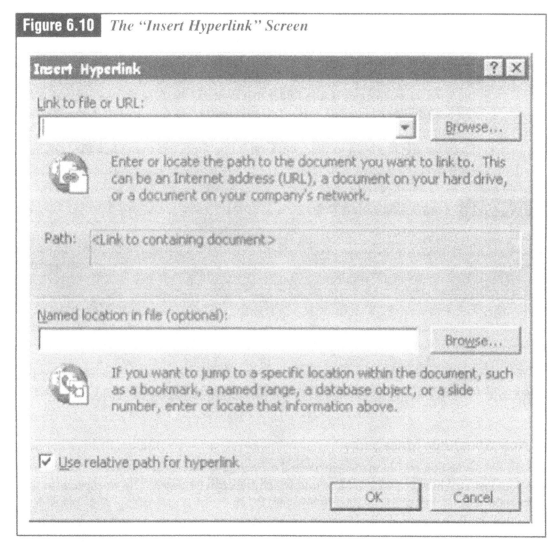

Microsoft® Word 2000 screen shot reprinted by permission from Microsoft Corporation.

Linking Pages in Your Web Project Using MS Word 2000

As the activities in the Web-based learning framework grow in complexity, the need to be able to create multiple Web pages that link to one another becomes apparent. Just as the Web page storyboard illustrated, a teacher's Web page or activity typically involves a home page with several subordinate pages. In this case, a teacher can create all of the files associated with a specific activity and save them all to one folder on the hard drive of a computer, a floppy disk, or a network drive. Placing all of the files in one folder makes creating consistent links much easier. Eventually, when all of the Web pages that constitute an activity are posted on the Internet, the activity should enable users to click on hyperlinks that transport them to each page in the activity. The following steps outline how to link together the various Web pages in an activity.

1. Highlight a word or line of text on a page that users should click on to take them to a new page in the activity. For example, if the first page of an activity were the Introduction page, there might be a link on the page that when clicked on transports the user to a new page that explains the assessment for the activity. It could be something as basic as:

"Please click <u>here</u> to view the assessment for this activity."

2. Locate and click on the "Insert" menu and then select the "Hyperlink" submenu.
3. Click on the "Browse" button. This will list the folders and files on the computer. Locating the document involves using the drop-down arrow near the top of the window to navigate to the folder that contains the files that were created for the activity. *(For help with this, please review the section on File Management in Chapter 4.)*
4. Once the file has been located, click on it one time, and then click the "OK" button.

| Figure 6.11 | *Linking to a Web Page* |

Microsoft® Internet Explorer 5.0 screen shot reprinted by permission from Microsoft Corporation.

A Note About File Management

Recall the discussion on file management in the Chapter 4 Technical Corner. In that section, we demonstrated how to create folders into which files can be saved. This is especially important when it comes to creating Web pages. When creating and saving Web pages, it is vital that the Web page and all of its components (pictures, graphics, sounds) be saved in the same folder. This is necessary because each of the items like pictures and graphics, are separate files that are inserted into a Web page. When the Web page is displayed in a Web browser, it searches for any pictures or graphics in the folder in which the Web page is saved. (Exceptions to this exist, but to keep things simple, make sure to save the Web page and all of its components in the same folder). Additionally, when getting ready to post a Web page on a Web site or on a district Web server, it is much easier when all of the files are in the same place.

Posting Web Pages to a Web Site

Posting an activity on the Internet is the one of the crowning moments in any teacher's technical training. It is the moment when all of your hard work goes "live" for the rest of the world to use. Many districts now have their own Web servers (computers that host a Web site) on which teachers' work can be posted. Additionally, there are multitudes of both commercial and non-commercial Web sites that will host Web pages. There is no single right way to post your work. Some basic guidelines to make posting a Web page a little less confusing are as follows:

1. Save a Web page(s) on a hard drive or on a floppy disk. Locate and click on the desired file to load it into the Web browser.
2. Contact your Webmaster or system administrator to arrange to have your Web page posted on the school district's Web site.
3. Use a free page service.
4. Free Web space may be available through your commercial provider as part of your service fee.

A useful Web site to use to begin identifying ways to post your Web page or Web site is <**http://www.buddyproject.org/tool/design/1hosting.asp**>. At this site, several suggestions are provided explaining different options for posting material. Fortunately, most of them are free to educators. Some of these sites include: <**http://myschoolonline.com/**>, <**http://www.homestead.com/**>, <**http://schools.bigchalk.com/**>, and <**http://www.school-center.com/**>. Other sites that allow you to post a Web site free include:

Free Yellow <**http://www.webpages4free.freeyellow.com/**>
Tripod <**www.tripod.com/**>
Geocities <**http://www.geocities.com/)**>
Web 66 <**http://Web66.coled.umn.edu/**>
SchoolNotes.com <**http://www.SchoolNotes.com**>
Homeroom.net <**http://www.homeroom.net**>
SNET Free School Web Hosting <**http://www.snetWeb.com/school/index.shtml**>

Additionally, because hyperlinks are constantly changing, teachers also can select their favorite search engine and do a search for "free Web hosting sites." For example, using Google <**http://www.google.com/**>, the search may appear as shown in Figure 6.12.

Figure 6.12 *Locating Free Web Hosting Sites*

Screen shot reprinted with permission from Google, Inc.

After clicking on the "Google Search" button, you can then explore the hits that were returned that matched your search.

Figure 6.13 *Hits for Free Web Hosting Sites*

Screen shot reprinted with permission from Google, Inc.

Chapter 8 Technical Corner

Multi-Tasking

At this point, you aleady will have learned that throughout many of these activities, the teacher selects links, creates a Web page using those links, and then directs students to complete the assignment. But how do those links get to the Web page? What is the easiest, quickest way to do this? Based on the first few sections, many of the skills required to create a CyberInquiry are at your fingertips.

From this point forward, we will be working between two or more programs at the same time, which is called *multi-tasking*. This allows us to minimize a program we have open and work in a different program at the same time. This saves the time of closing one program, opening a different program, then re-opening the program we closed. This is done so that we can browse the Internet, copy URLs for our CyberInquiry, and then paste the URLs into our Web pages.

How to Multi-Task

1. Locate and run your Internet browser.
2. Minimize the browser by clicking on the "minus" symbol in the top right-hand corner of your window.

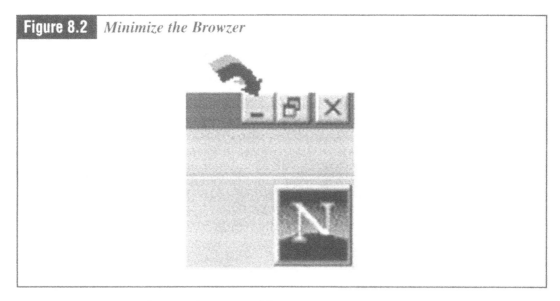

Figure 8.2 *Minimize the Browzer*

Netscape® Composer 4.5 screen shot reprinted by permission from Netscape Communications Corporations.

3. Locate and run the program that will be used to author Web pages. Remember to follow the directions for saving and naming your Web page.
4. Notice that the Internet browser is still running, but it is minimized in the form of an icon at the bottom of the screen.

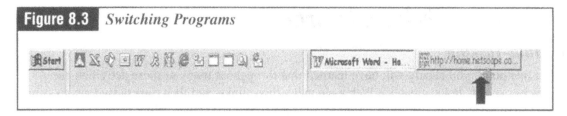

Figure 8.3 *Switching Programs*

Microsoft® Windows 2000 screen shot reprinted by permission from Microsoft Corporation.
Netscape® Composer 4.5 screen shot reprinted by permission from Netscape Communications
Corporation.

5. To switch between programs, just click on the icon of the program in which you wish to work.
6. Switch to the Internet browser and navigate to a URL from your "Favorites" or use a search engine. Highlight and copy the URL from the address box, switch back to the word processor and, paste the URL.

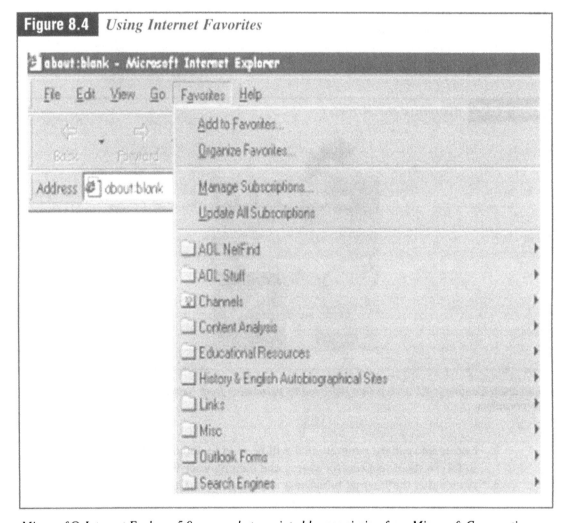

Figure 8.4 *Using Internet Favorites*

Microsoft® Internet Explorer 5.0 screen shot reprinted by permission from Microsoft Corporation.

Chapter 9 Technical Corner

Up to this point, we have demonstrated the fundamental skills required to design a WebQuest. With knowledge of copying and pasting, word processing, and some Web page skills, even a less-experienced computer user could create a WebQuest. This section explores a few more advanced options, such as linking to sound and video files when creating pages in any of the Web-based learning activities.

Using Sound in Web Pages

Sounds, whether music, special effects, or narratives, add a unique dimension to a Web page. However, they should be used only when the purpose is to help convey the content. Sound files for use in Web pages come from various sources, including commercially produced CD-ROMs, original recordings, and music CDs, as well as the Internet. When using any sound file, all applicable copyright guidelines should be followed. The following steps explain how to download a sound found on the Web and link to it within a Web page. Review search techniques *(see Chapter 5)* to see how to use search engines effectively to locate material. To download a sound file from the Web do the following:

1. Open your Internet browser.
2. Locate a Web site that has sounds or music files to use for a Web page.
3. An easy way to begin downloading a sound file is to right-click on the link and choose "Save Target As" from the menu.

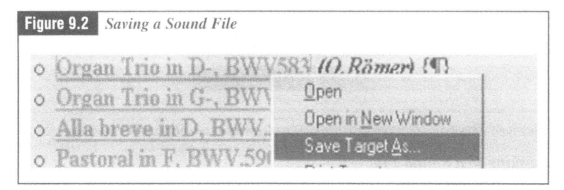

Figure 9.2 *Saving a Sound File*

Microsoft® Internet Explorer 5.0 screen shot reprinted by permission from Microsoft Corporation.

4. Choose to save the sound file in the same folder as the Web page in which it will be used.

Figure 9.3	*Choosing a Location*

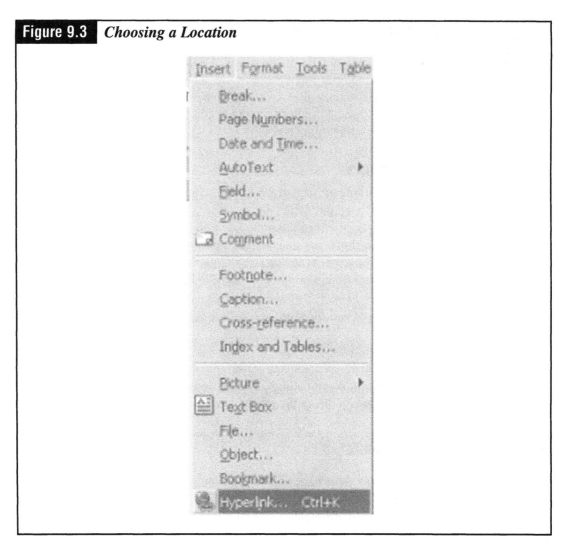

Microsoft® Windows 2000 screen shot reprinted by permission from Microsoft Corporation.

Linking to a Sound File

1. Open your Web-authoring program. (This example will use MS Word 2000.)
2. Open an existing Web page or create a new Web page.
3. Place text in the Web page that tells the user about the availability of a sound file. For example:

Click here to listen to Bach's Organ Trio in D-

4. Click and drag to highlight any portion of the text to insert a hyperlink.
5. Choose "Insert" and then "Hyperlink," and then browse to the location of the sound file.

| Figure 9.4 | *Creating a Link to a Sound File* |

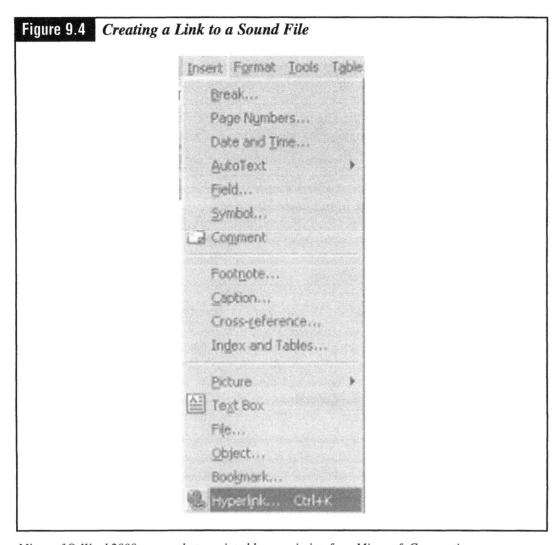

Microsoft® Word 2000 screen shot reprinted by permission from Microsoft Corporation.

6. The text will now be linked to the sound file.

| Figure 9.5 | *Locating the Sound File* |

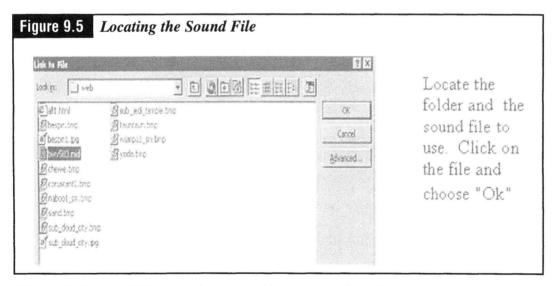

Locate the folder and the sound file to use. Click on the file and choose "Ok"

Microsoft® Windows 2000 screen shot reprinted by permission from Microsoft Corporation.

Plug-Ins and Add-Ins

Plug-ins/Add-ins are specific programs that allow special types of files to work in a Web browser. There are a multitude of plug-ins for various sound, graphic, and video files. Typically, to download a plug-in, one would navigate to the appropriate Web site and follow the directions for downloading the plug-in. This generally requires saving the plug-in file to your computer and running the file. The plug-in will then install itself and be available for use. The following are some common plug-ins and the sites from which they can be downloaded.

- Real Player® – Plays variety of music and video file formats
  **http://www.real.com/products/player/downloadrealplayer.html?
  wp=dl1099&src=hp_butn,home&lang=en**

- Shockwave® – Plays hundreds of multimedia files commonly found on the Internet, such as advertisements, games, and business presentations
  http://www.shockwave.com/

- Adobe Acrobat Reader® – Allows users to view files created with Adobe Acrobat, which is used widely on the Internet as a universal document format
  http://www.adobe.com/products/acrobat/readstep.html

- Quicktime Player® – Plays streaming video over the Internet
  http://www.apple.com/quicktime/

Web-Based Learning: A Practical Guide

H

I

J

K

L

M

N

O

P